LATIN AMERICA
From Colonization
to Globalization

LATIN AMERICA
From Colonization
to Globalization

Noam Chomsky
in conversation with Heinz Dieterich

OCEAN PRESS
Melbourne • New York

Cover design by David Spratt

ISBN 1-876175-13-3

First printed 1999

Printed in Australia

Published by Ocean Press
Australia: GPO Box 3279, Melbourne, Victoria 3001, Australia
• Fax: (61-3) 9372 1765 • E-mail: ocean_press@msn.com.au
USA: PO Box 834, Hoboken, NJ 07030 • Fax: 201-617 0203

Library of Congress Catalog Card No: 99-070348

Translations by Roque Grillo, Diane Chomsky and Moisés Espinoza

OCEAN PRESS DISTRIBUTORS
United States: LPC/InBook,
        1436 West Randolph St, Chicago, IL 60607, USA
Canada: Login Brothers
        324 Salteaux Cres, Winnipeg, Manitoba R3J, Canada
Britain and Europe: Global Book Marketing,
        38 King Street, London, WC2E 8JT, UK
Australia and New Zealand: Astam Books,
        57-61 John Street, Leichhardt, NSW 2040, Australia
Cuba and Latin America: Ocean Press,
        Calle 21 #406, Vedado, Havana, Cuba
Southern Africa: Phambili Agencies,
        PO Box 28680, Kensington 2101, Johannesburg, South Africa

CONTENTS

Preface

It is 20 years since the Nicaraguan revolution swept the Sandinistas to power, presenting the people of Latin America with a fragile glimmer of hope in an otherwise horrendous period. Against tremendous odds the new government pursued an ambitious program of social and economic development, increasing spending on health and education and carrying out extensive land reform.[1] The following report, based on an interview with Esmilda Flores, a peasant woman living on a cooperative, captures something of the spirit unleashed by the Sandinistas' victory:

> "Before the revolution, we didn't participate in anything. We only learned to make tortillas and cook beans and do what our husbands told us. In only five years we've seen a lot of changes — and we're still working on it!" Esmilda Flores belongs to an agricultural cooperative in the mountains north of Estelí, Nicaragua. Together with seven other women and fifteen men, she works land that was formerly a coffee plantation owned by an absentee landlord. After the revolution in 1979, the families who had worked the land became its owners. They have expanded production to include corn, beans, potatoes, cabbages, and dairy cows. "Before, we had to rent a small plot to grow any food," Flores said, "and we had to pay one-half of our crop to the landlord! Now we work just as hard as before — both in the fields and at home — but there's a difference, because we're working for ourselves…"[2]

After returning from a trip to Nicaragua in 1986, Chomsky described it as "one of the few places where a decent person can live with a certain sense of integrity and hope."[3] For the United States, however, Nicaragua's "integrity and hope" posed a threat which demanded a severe response — "a country of this sort is an enemy," Chomsky noted.[4] For more than a decade, the United States waged a bitter war against people like Esmilda Flores throughout Latin America. Several hundred thousand people were killed.[5]

Throughout this period, as Chomsky and Edward Herman have extensively documented, the U.S. propaganda system attempted to hide the true nature and significance of these battles from the public.[6] Thus, when the Sandinistas finally lost power in the 1990 elections, the U.S. media recorded the event as a victory for burgeoning Latin American democracy, notwithstanding the fact that "the U.S. government repeatedly announced that if their favored party, the UNO coalition, did not win, the economic embargo, which had already caused $3 billion worth of damage, would continue, as would U.S. sponsorship of Contra terrorism."[7] Similar U.S.-sponsored "free and fair" elections were held in El Salvador and Guatemala, and were greeted with acclaim by dutiful media.[8]

In the face of such systematic distortions of history, this collection of eleven interviews with Noam Chomsky is particularly valuable. Chomsky has spent a good part of his life helping to "counter the deluge of propaganda" by exposing the truth about U.S. policy in Latin America and elsewhere.[9] Among Chomsky's many works on Latin America, this collection is unusual in that the interviews span a period of 14 years, allowing the reader a glimpse at the issues which preoccupied activists at different times from 1984 to 1998 — from the height of the Contra insurgency and Reagan's new Cold War to the devastation of the Asian economic crisis and the renewed U.S. assault on Cuba. More importantly, perhaps, the interviews stress the continuity of the colonial process, from 1492 to the present day, from Columbus to Clinton. This emphasis on persistent themes is one of the hallmarks of Chomsky's analysis of U.S. foreign policy. His position is summed up well by the following extract from a lecture he delivered at the Universidad Centroamericana in Managua in 1986:[10]

> What the United States is doing today in Central America is not at all new, and it is not specific to Latin America. We mislead ourselves by viewing these matters in too narrow a focus, as is commonly done in journalism and much of scholarship, both in the United States and elsewhere.
>
> Surveying the historical record, we do find some variation in U.S. policies. The continuities, however, are much more striking than the variation, which reflects tactical judgments and estimates of feasibility. The persistent and largely invariant features of U.S. foreign

policy are deeply rooted in the domestic society of the United States. These factors determine a restricted framework of policy formation that admits few departures.

Planning and action are based on principles and geopolitical analyses that are often spelled out rather clearly in internal documents. They are also revealed with much clarity by the historical record. If these principles are understood, then we can comprehend quite well what the United States is doing in the world. We can also understand a good deal of contemporary history, given the power and influence of the United States. Current U.S. policies in Central America also fall into place, fitting historical patterns that change very little because of the relatively constant nexus of interests and power from which they arise.[11]

Chomsky goes on to explain the principles which have animated U.S. foreign policy since its inception. His discussion of the first of these principles is worth extracting at length since it encapsulates one of the major themes in this collection of interviews and, indeed, in Chomsky's other political writings.

The first principle is that U.S. foreign policy is designed to create and maintain an international order in which U.S.-based business can prosper, a world of "open societies," meaning societies that are open to profitable investment, to expansion of export markets and transfer of capital, and to exploitation of material and human resources on the part of U.S. corporations and their local affiliates. "Open societies," in the true meaning of the term, are societies that are open to U.S. economic penetration and political control.

Preferably, these "open societies" should have parliamentary democratic forms, but this is a distinctly secondary consideration. Parliamentary forms... are tolerable only as long as economic, social and ideological institutions, and the coercive forces of the state, are firmly in the hands of groups that can be trusted to act in general accord with the needs of those who own and manage U.S. society. If this condition is satisfied, then parliamentary forms in some client states are a useful device, ensuring the dominance of minority elements favored by U.S. elites while enabling the U.S. political leadership to mobilize its own population in support of foreign adventures masked in idealistic rhetoric ("defense of democracy") but undertaken for quite different purposes. In its actual usage, the term "democracy," in U.S. rhetoric, refers to a system of governance in which elite elements based in the business community control the state by virtue of their dominance of private society, while the population observes quietly. So understood, democracy is a system of elite decision and public ratification, as in the United States itself.

Correspondingly, popular involvement in the formation of public policy is considered a serious threat. It is not a step towards democracy; rather it constitutes a "crisis of democracy" that must be overcome. The problem arises both in the United States and in its dependencies, and has been addressed by measures ranging from public relations campaigns to death squads, depending on which population is targeted...

What all of this means for much of the third world, to put it crudely but accurately, is that the primary concern of U.S. foreign policy is to guarantee the freedom to rob and exploit.

Elsewhere, I have referred to this as "the Fifth Freedom," one that was not enunciated by President Franklin Delano Roosevelt when he formulated the famous Four Freedoms, which were presented as the war aims of the Western allies during World War II: Freedom of Speech, Freedom of Worship, Freedom from Want, and Freedom from Fear. The history of Central America and the Caribbean — and not these regions alone — reveals just how these fine words are to be understood: as a means to gain public support for crusades in defense of the Fifth Freedom, the one that really counts.[12]

Yet, despite the apparently awesome power of the propaganda system, "public support" for U.S. "crusades" is not always forthcoming. In this collection, and elsewhere, Chomsky emphasizes the crucial role which domestic dissent can play in constraining U.S. terror. In Chomsky's view, U.S. intervention in Latin America during the 1980s might have been even more devastating without the widespread popular opposition that emerged: "What took place is bad enough. B-52 bombing would have been worse, much worse."[13]

This collection, and Chomsky's other writings, are not a counsel of despair, but a call to action accompanied by a message of cautious hope:

... I just try to describe as best I can what I think is happening. When you look at that, it's not very pretty, and if you extrapolate it into the future, it's very ugly.

But the point is... *it's not inevitable.* The future can be changed. But we can't change things unless we at least begin to understand them.[14]

* * * * * * * * * *

This collection of interviews is based on an earlier Spanish edition which was published as *Noam Chomsky habla de América Latina* by Casa Editora Abril, Havana, 1998. Unfortunately, the original transcripts of some of the interviews were unavailable for use in the preparation of this edition of the collection. Consequently, the interviews included in chapters one, six, seven, eight and nine had to be translated from Spanish to English. This task was skillfully performed by Roque Grillo. Diane Chomsky and Moisés Espinoza also assisted with translation. The editors would like to thank Noam Chomsky for reading the final version of the manuscript and making some valuable corrections.

The editors have included explanatory notes which appear as footnotes to the interviews. Noam Chomsky and Heinz Dieterich are not responsible for any errors that may appear in the explanatory notes or the Preface. The quotations which appear at the beginning of each of the interviews were selected by the editors from a variety of works by Noam Chomsky and, in one case, from a work co-written by Noam Chomsky and Edward Herman.

Julian Sempill and Denise Glasbeek
July 1999

Introduction
Noam Chomsky on the Liberation of Latin America

If you assume that there is no hope, you guarantee that there will be no hope. If you assume that there is an instinct for freedom, that there are opportunities to change things, then there is a possibility that you can contribute to making a better world. That's your choice.

Noam Chomsky

There is no better way to sum up Noam Chomsky's philosophy of life. In this capitalist world where our youth's best talents are consumed by the neoliberal creed that the meaning of life resides in acquiring business, purchasing and political power, the scientist's pronouncement is a light in the darkness. Not only for its inherent ethical value, but also for the degree to which its author has put his beliefs into practice.

In this sense, it is no exaggeration to speak of Chomsky's philosophy of praxis, even if he never intentionally elaborated one as such. Just as Marx's logic of the social sciences was never explicitly written up but is present throughout his work, so Noam Chomsky's philosophy of praxis penetrates all his writings. It centers on three necessary imperatives for the democratic society of the future. First: to put an end to exploitation and economic inequality, this society must be anticapitalist; second: to put an end to political elitism and create a participatory democracy, the society must be non-statist; and third: to ensure the enlightenment of all citizens, all feudal and pre-industrial structures must be eliminated. This architecture will guarantee that the new society's ultimate aim is reached: the personal realization of each individual citizen.

Based on this philosophy of praxis, Noam Chomsky provides us with the epistemological and political keys to the liberation of our

America: a scientific understanding of the history of Latin America and the history of the United States. Chomsky destroys the enslaving power that the word wields in the myths of domination by the American elite, and restores its liberating force through reason. Faced with his analysis, the chains of propaganda fall to pieces and the real cause-and-effect relations in the politics of the system's rulers are revealed, rebelling against the doctrinaire strait-jacket which suffocates them.

Therefore, this work is more than a living memory of recent decades of the empire's foreign policy; it is a reminder and an appeal to acknowledge once again the systematic place that Latin American and U.S. history occupy in the liberation of *La Patria Grande* [the Great Motherland of the Americas]. They are a prism revealing the logic behind the elite's behavior, which represents the key to Latin America's anti-democracy and misery since the wars of independence against Spanish colonialism. Without understanding this logic there will be no chance of "contributing to make a better world" in *La Patria Grande*.

Noam Chomsky's reasoning leads to profound questions. For example, how long can a national-popular project survive the subversive and destabilizing efforts of the White House, under a bourgeois democracy? Jacobo Arbenz's government in Guatemala lasted only three years (1951–54) before it was overthrown by a U.S. coup d'état; the Salvador Allende government lasted two-and-a-half years (1970–73) before suffering the same fate; the Sandinista revolution resisted for six years (1984–90) and the Bolivian revolution held out for 12 years (1952–64) before being overthrown by a Washington coup d'état.

The time differences among these examples are due to a simple fact: Allende and Arbenz controlled governments but not the state, while the Sandinistas and Bolivians controlled both elements of power, thus prolonging the White House's subversive work. In light of these reflections, the Cuban experience — resisting 39 years of U.S. aggression — acquires dimensions beyond those that arise from a simple abstract reflection on the desirability and undesirability of Latin America's bourgeois democratic and socialist structures.

Another example that compels us to reflect is the following: when Salvador Allende won the elections in 1970, the Nixon-Kissinger government tried to prevent the democratically elected president from taking and maintaining power. But it was not possible for Washington to arrange a "preventive" military coup due to what the CIA referred to in its secret documents as the "constitutionalist inertia" of the Chilean armed forces. The White House needed three years to destroy the economy of the country and organize a pro-coup faction that would end the popular regime. In order not to repeat that experience, the United States is currently forming pro-coup factions — using the absurd pretext of the war against drug barons — so that "preventive" coups d'état can occur rapidly whenever needed to destroy democratic governability by neoliberalism.

The German philosopher Schelling used to say that the "beginning and end of philosophy is freedom," warning that "human beings are born to act and not to speculate." Chomsky complies with both imperatives and this gives him a place in the ranks of the great thinkers and liberators of *La Patria Grande*, from José Martí and Manuela Saénz to Che Guevara.

Heinz Dieterich

1

1492: The First Invasion of Globalization

The discovery of America, and that of a passage to the East Indies by the Cape of Good Hope, are the two greatest and most important events recorded in the history of mankind... the new set of exchanges... should naturally have proved as advantageous to the new, as it certainly did to the old continent... The savage injustice of the Europeans rendered an event, which ought to have been beneficial to all, ruinous and destructive to several of those unfortunate countries.

Adam Smith, 1776[1]

I believe that because of these impious, criminal and ignominious deeds perpetrated so unjustly, tyrannically and barbarously, God will vent upon Spain His wrath and His fury, for nearly all of Spain has shared in the bloody wealth usurped at the cost of so much ruin and slaughter.

Statement from the will of Las Casas,
a 16th century Spanish writer[2]

I think that it's not asking too much to have our little region over here [namely, Latin America] which never has bothered anybody.

Henry Stimson, U.S. Secretary of War, 1945[3]

---

* These interviews were conducted between October 1989 and March 1992.

Heinz Dieterich: 1992 is the 500th anniversary of Columbus's voyage to the Americas. Official celebrations speak of the "fifth centenary of the discovery of America" and of the "meeting of two cultures." Are these appropriate ways to refer to this event?

Noam Chomsky: There's no doubt that there was a meeting of two worlds. But the phrase "discovery of America" is obviously inaccurate. What they discovered was an America that had been discovered thousands of years before by its inhabitants. Thus, what took place was the *invasion* of America — an invasion by a very alien culture.

HD: So, indigenous peoples are correct when they refer to it as the "conquest" or the "invasion"?

NC: Obviously. One can discover an uninhabited area, but not one in which people live. If I travel to Mexico, I can't write an article entitled "The Discovery of Mexico."

HD: Is October 12, 1492, a date that should be celebrated? [This is commonly accepted as the date of Columbus's arrival in the Americas].

NC: Well, I do think that people should pay attention to it; it is an extremely important date in modern history. In fact, there are few events in modern history that have had such formidable implications. In statistical terms alone — which don't often say much about reality — a century and a half after the conquest almost 100 million human beings had disappeared.

It is difficult to think of comparable events in human history. The effects of the conquest did, of course, dramatically change the Western hemisphere and, as a result, Western civilization. Thus, it is undoubtedly a very important turning point in world history. Nevertheless, "celebrate" is a strange word. I don't think that we would "celebrate" Hitler's coming to power, for example, even if we certainly do pay attention to it.

HD: When Columbus reached the Western hemisphere, he called the inhabitants "Indians" because he thought he was in the Indies. Five hundred years after this geographical error was clarified, these people are still being called "Indians." Why?

NC: Well, I think that this reflects the general contempt for indigenous peoples. If they didn't really have any right to be where they were, it also would have mattered little what they were called. The conquerors equally could have called the animals that they found here by the wrong name and no one would have been overly troubled by it.

The situation varied throughout the continent. So, for example, in areas where the English settled or where English is spoken today, the unwritten law in force in England was imposed. According to English law, the inhabitants of these lands didn't have a right to them because they where hunter-gatherers rather than a sedentary people. This was completely false. And many other falsifications of events took place in order to render them compatible with the law.

Up until the 1970s, for example, distinguished anthropologists informed us that we should reject archeological and documentary evidence which clearly showed that these were sedentary peoples and, by their own standards, relatively advanced civilizations. On the contrary, we were to pretend that they were hunter-gatherers and that, therefore, there were few people, maybe a million north of the Rio Grande, instead of 10 million or more, which was the real figure.

And if the question is asked why for centuries these falsifications were made, the answer is, basically, that it was a matter of establishing the principle that the people who lived there had no rights over the land, given that they simply traveled across it in order to hunt, and so on. Therefore, there was no moral or legal problem in taking their land for the use of the Europeans. As far as the peoples involved are concerned, if they had no right to the land, it did not matter who they were, or whether they came from India or some other place.

As a result of events that took place in the 1960s, there has been a kind of cultural change in the last 20 years. Most of what happened in the 1960s was extremely healthy and significant. It became possible, for the first time, to face the questions about what had been done to the native American population. This produced a degree of consciousness about the racist nature of our willingness to continue to use terms such as "Indians," as if who they were was of no importance.

HD: What is the appropriate way for people in the solidarity movements to approach 1992?

NC: Well, I think that the approach of the solidarity movements should be, above all, to honestly face up to the events and to have a clear understanding of them. And, to take advantage of the occasion so that the events relating to the European invasion of the Western hemisphere and the consequences of what took place become known, including the situation and treatment of the indigenous people — all those massacres and the oppression of the indigenous peoples that began in 1492 and continues to this day.

All one needs to do is look at what is taking place in Guatemala, or in the reservations of western United States, or throughout the hemisphere to realize that persecution and repression continue under our noses, frequently in brutal form.

Gaining an understanding of what these last 500 years have meant is not simply a matter of becoming aware of history, it is a question of becoming aware of current processes. I think that the solidarity movement should attempt to reach, for itself and for others, an understanding of these events and attempt to establish a base from which it can understand them honestly and humanely for the first time.

HD: After 1492, the peoples of Latin America were integrated into the world system, as dependants. Have they managed to recover their autonomy?

NC: No. The relationship between the invaders and the indigenous population differs from place to place in America. In some areas, the indigenous people were integrated in some form and in others they were simply eliminated or displaced, or put into reservations. Relations vary, but the end result of all this is that the majority of the hemisphere still finds itself subjugated.

For reasons that have to do with world history, the English-speaking parts became dominant world powers, particularly the United States, which is the first truly global power in history. Latin America has been subordinated to the Western imperial powers and their violence. And this continues. It continues in the foreign debt crisis, in the threats of intervention, in the highly distorted forms of development, in the frequently extreme social backwardness of many areas that have great cultural wealth. These are all phenomena that have developed in the course of international relations and they have, for various reasons, led to a highly dependent, subjugated and oppressive situation for the majority of the continent.

1992 should also lead us, and perhaps it will, to consider the current form of domination in the international sphere. It doesn't have all the forms of traditional colonialism, but it manifests other features that should be unacceptable to any honest person. Frequently, it has terrible consequences. It should suffice to look at events in Central America during the past decade to see how serious these effects can be.

HD: In light of the mistreatment suffered by the indigenous people of the United States, how can you explain President Reagan becoming defender of the indigenous Miskitu people of Nicaragua? NC: Remember that Reagan — and not only him but the whole of the U.S. ideological apparatus — defended, or pretended to defend them, and appeared very annoyed by what was happening to them. At the same time, Reagan and the people around him applauded what was happening in Guatemala. Not only did he defend it, he applauded and rallied support for it. In 1982, Reagan explained that the dictator Ríos Montt [1982–83] was a man dedicated to democracy and we heard similar things from Jeane Kirkpatrick,[4] and the rest of that gang.

During that whole period, George Shultz,[5] Elliot Abrams,[6] Reagan allies and many others defended and supported events in Guatemala, and never seriously protested about what was happening there. Meanwhile, they acted like they were preoccupied with the fate of the Miskitus. The Miskitus were mistreated, but nevertheless found themselves among the best treated indigenous groups in the hemisphere. If the obviously very legitimate demands they made in relation to their autonomy from the Sandinista government had taken place in any country to the north of Nicaragua, these people would have simply been massacred (had ridicule of their demands not been sufficient).

Reagan and the State Department talk of the barbaric and inhumane treatment of the Miskitus (possibly several dozen of them had died in conflict with the Sandinistas). But at the same time, some 70,000 or 80,000 people were massacred in the Guatemalan high plateau by the armed forces, who were supported by the United States and defended by Ronald Reagan as very good and honest people who cared about democracy. To this day, it's still claimed that the Guatemalan military were unjustly accused.

If we take a look at the treatment of the native peoples of the United States, then the treatment of the Miskitus appears very respectful by comparison. In fact, if any group of native Americans in the United States expressed similar demands for autonomy, and ridicule was insufficient to neutralize them, then they would simply be annihilated. That is why no one can consider this to be anything more than the most extraordinary of hypocrisies by the U.S. government.

HD: Historically, the native peoples of the United States have occupied the lowest place in the scale of social and ethnic status in their country. Has this situation changed in recent times?

NC: Yes, it has changed. I clearly remember when I was a child the favorite game for young people was "Cowboys and Indians." You went to the forest and pretended that there were "Indians." It was like going hunting, like hunting animals. Popular culture back then emphasized the concept of the "Indian" as a treacherous savage, or perhaps, a noble savage, who led a primitive life before achieving the higher level of civilization of the Europeans. Well, this has certainly changed, that is, the vulgar racism that existed until the 1960s has changed. And this, again, was a result of the impact of the 1960s and the significant improvement of cultural and moral standards that took place during that time. On the other hand, native Americans are still treated abominably. If you want an example of this, look at Ward Churchill's excellent book *Agents of Repression*, which deals with the war by the FBI against the American Indian Movement. This is a very concrete example and, what's more, it concerns recent events, events that took place in the 1960s.

HD: So, native Americans continue to be at the bottom of the racial prejudice scale?

NC: Yes, by many standards they occupy the lowest point and, in fact, they are virtually considered nonexistent.

HD: Some have proposed bringing the statue of Columbus from Barcelona to New York to "marry" it to the Statue of Liberty as part of the 1992 celebrations. What do you think of this idea?

NC: Columbus was one of the main specialists in genocide during that period. Also, and leaving aside for a moment his abominable practices, the symbolism is offensive because his voyages to the Western hemisphere began a period in which a population of tens of millions was, essentially, annihilated. To call this liberty goes far beyond anything George Orwell could ever have imagined.

HD: Carlos Fuentes was asked in Santiago de Chile what he thought about the great statue of the Spanish conquistador Pedro de Valdivia. His answer was: "I hoped for more statues of Cortés in Mexico so that we could rid ourselves of the complex of having been colonized." This answer seems very strange to me. What do you think about it?

NC: Well, I also think it is a strange answer. I can't understand it. I'd like to ask him what it means to him. But it is very strange. When he said that "we" were colonized, who was he talking about? Who was colonized? Was *he* colonized by Spain? In the same way that the United States was colonized by England? He is a descendant of the

conquerors. The indigenous population was overwhelmingly eliminated. And he is saying that we should honor the murderers? I
don't quite understand it.

HD: I think he is talking about the people who are protesting
against the Fifth Centenary celebrations, because here they say that
the people who protest against these celebrations have a complex:
they can't get past what took place 500 years ago. I think that's
more or less the meaning.

NC: What happened 500 years ago is, of course, still happening
now. The main theme of the last 500 years of human history, and
this hasn't changed, is what today is called the North–South
conflict, essentially the European conquest of the world. If he wants
to forget this, he wants to forget reality. If the "complex" is
recognizing the reality in which we live, then yes, I understand,
because one of the principal tasks of intellectuals has always been to
get past this "complex," but I would not have expected it from him.

HD: Many apologists for the Fifth Centenary celebrations say that
the Spanish brought civilization with them — and, in particular,
"the marvelous language of Cervantes" — and insinuate that due to
this incomparable language it was all worth it, in spite of some
atrocities taking place.

NC: I don't know the Nazi period well enough to know if someone
said that the Germans took the marvelous language of Goethe to the
ghettos of Warsaw, but if this was the case, then it would be a
comparable statement.

HD: A similar statement has been made by people who say "while
there were sorrows, they are compensated for by the coming of the
Christian faith."

NC: I can give you the same analogy. The Germans took Christian
faith to the ghettos of Warsaw.

HD: For 150 years, the people who have lived in this part of the
continent have considered themselves citizens of Latin America.
When the Spanish introduced a lot of money because of the Fifth
Centenary, many journalists and intellectuals discovered that this is
"Ibero-America." How can a bit of money make such a change
possible after 150 years?

NC: The answer is in the question. People have a price, some will
sell themselves for five cents, others will ask a million dollars.

HD: We are building a "Monument to the victims of the European
invasion of 1492" in the Spanish city of Puerto Real, together with
the city's council and independent Spanish groups. The famous

Ecuadorian artist Osvaldo Guyasamin is designing it. The socialist government of Felipe González tried to silence this. And now they are distributing a letter to the citizens of Puerto Real with the aim of collecting signatures in order to dismiss the mayor. They justify this campaign by claiming that the monument is a monument to hatred and not to reconciliation. What is your opinion of this?

NC: The conquerors don't want the truth to be known — not only that Spain conquered large parts of the Western hemisphere, but also that they benefited from it, and still do. As I have said, the oft-mentioned North–South conflict, the European conquest of the world, continues. Right now, Latin America is being subjugated. The social and economic structural adjustment is only a modern phase of the massacres of indigenous people.

HD: This is because an innocent action like the building of a monument...

NC: There's nothing "innocent" about it. Anything that generates consciousness and understanding among the poor people of the world is not innocent.

HD: It's dangerous?

NC: Very dangerous, that's understood.

HD: So we are a dangerous species?

NC: Absolutely. That's why they sent the prophets into the desert thousands of years ago.

2

Latin America and the Vietnam War Syndrome

... we have about 50 percent of the world's wealth, but only 6.3 percent of its population... In this situation, we cannot fail to be the object of envy and resentment. Our real task in the coming period is to devise a pattern of relationships which will permit us to maintain this position of disparity without positive detriment to our national security. To do so, we will have to dispense with all sentimentality and day-dreaming; and our attention will have to be concentrated everywhere on our immediate national objectives. We need not deceive ourselves that we can afford today the luxury of altruism and world-benefaction... We should cease to talk about vague and — for the Far East — unreal objectives such as human rights, the raising of living standards, and democratization. The day is not far off when we are going to have to deal in straight power concepts. The less we are then hampered by idealistic slogans, the better.

George Kennan, Policy Planning Study 23,
U.S. State Department, 1948 [1]

The final answer might be an unpleasant one, but... we should not hesitate before police repression by the local government. This is not shameful since the Communists are essentially traitors... It is better to have a strong regime in power than a liberal government if it is indulgent and relaxed and penetrated by Communists.

George Kennan, in a briefing
for Latin American ambassadors 1950 [2]

---

* This interview was conducted in May 1984.

The [Salvadoran] death squads did exactly what they were supposed to do: they decapitated the trade unions and mass organizations that seemed in danger of setting off an urban insurrection at the beginning of the decade... [The army] learnt its tricks at American counterinsurgency schools in Panama and the United States. "We learnt from you," a death squad member once told an American reporter, "we learnt from you the methods, like blowtorches in the armpits, shots in the balls." And political prisoners often insist they were tortured by foreigners, some Argentine, others maybe American.

Ambrose Evans-Pritchard in *The Spectator*,
May 10, 1986[3]

... you may have to sell [intervention or other military actions] in such a way as to create the misimpression that it is the Soviet Union that you are fighting...

Professor Samuel Huntington, Harvard University[4]

Heinz Dieterich: Can the Central American conflict be compared to the Indochina conflict and, if so, in what respects?

Noam Chomsky: There are many differences, but there are also some striking similarities. It seems to me that the Central American conflict today is at the level of the Indochina conflict about 20 years ago. Let's take a look back at that. In the period from 1954 to 1960 — after the United States had taken over and had succeeded in undermining the possibility of a political settlement and had destroyed the Geneva agreements — the United States used, essentially, a local mercenary army in South Vietnam. It created a military force and it created the framework of a puppet government which, during those years, carried on an intensive assault against the population. The aim was to destroy the basis of the South Vietnamese nationalist movement, what we call the Vietcong, which was basically the southern branch of the *Vietminh* (the anti-French resistance movement).

The American government knew very well that as long as the Vietnamese nationalist movement survived, there was no hope of maintaining a client regime in South Vietnam. Thus, in the period from 1954 to 1960, extensive efforts were made to crush and destroy that movement and it was a very bloody period. There were thousands of political prisoners and many people were killed. The Vietnam scholar and military historian Bernard Fall reported that as many as 70,000 to 80,000 people were killed in counterinsurgency operations.

Up until 1959, the *Vietminh* was under orders not to use force in self-defense. The reason was that they were still hoping that the political settlement agreed upon in Geneva could somehow be carried out with elections and unification. But by 1959, it was clear that they were simply being decimated by the American-backed mercenary forces. Then they received authorization to use force in self-defense and, as soon as they did, the government and the military apparatus collapsed very quickly. In the early 1960s, the United States had to move to intervene directly. Thus, in 1961–62, the United States began direct bombing of rural South Vietnam and a few years later turned to direct invasion.

Turning to Central America, if we take the example of El Salvador, I would say that the period from 1979 – when the Romero government [1977–79] fell and the American intervention began extensively – was similar to South Vietnam in the late 1950s. In 1980, the assault on the population reached new heights of terror and violence and the major military assault against the peasantry began. It was a year in which there was a vast increase in state terrorism directed against the urban population with the purpose of breaking up and destroying the popular organizations. During the 1970s, a substantial network of popular organizations had been developed – peasant cooperatives, unions, church communities and so on and so forth. That network had to be destroyed prior to establishing the American-sponsored regime. So 1980 was primarily devoted to destroying the network of organizations of the political opposition, including the murder of the main political leaders in November.

The large-scale attack on the peasantry began in May 1980, the university was demolished in June and there was general repression intended to intimidate the population so that the United States could carry out some kind of fake elections and impose the typical Central America regime, organized by the United States along the standard lines.

That was in 1980 and it did work to a certain extent — in fact, it did succeed in virtually destroying the popular organizations, which were the basis for political opposition. But, while it did destroy the political opposition as a functioning group, it also created a guerrilla war. In early 1981, when the Reagan administration came in, they were faced with a problem very similar to that of the Kennedy administration 20 years earlier — the massive military and terrorist attacks against the political opposition had created a guerrilla war which they were unable to contain. Well, Kennedy moved on to direct American military intervention and Reagan has been trying to find a way to do the same. They've expanded the American military involvement in various ways and there is no doubt in my mind that Reagan would simply have intervened directly with military force in 1981, if he could have.

The major difference between the current period and the early 1960s is the attitude of the American population. When Kennedy and later Johnson escalated the war against South Vietnam and subsequently all Indochina, there was virtually no opposition. In 1961 and 1962, when the Kennedy administration began the large-scale bombing in South Vietnam, there was no opposition at all. Now every step in the escalation has met with quite considerable popular opposition and the administration has had to back off. That's El Salvador.

On the other hand, there's Nicaragua. The Carter administration supported Somoza until the very end. Then, the American-supported military intervention against the Sandinistas began immediately in 1979. But the Carter administration did attempt to find a way to support the more conservative and pro-American elements in the Sandinista coalition and bring them into power. The Reagan administration gave up that attempt and simply turned to war against Nicaragua. The United States built up a permanent military force, which is a strictly mercenary army. In fact, it is one of the largest and best equipped armies in Central America — with better and more advanced equipment than the Nicaraguan army itself. This mercenary force has been carrying out a war against Nicaragua, including, for example, the recent [U.S.] mining operations in Nicaraguan harbors.

Since there is no popular force within Nicaragua that is carrying out any substantial opposition to the regime, they have to attack the country from outside. The American government tries to compare the Nicaraguan situation with El Salvador, but there is no comparison at all. In El Salvador, we have a client government, supported from the outside, fighting its own population, whereas in the case of Nicaragua, it's a CIA-sponsored, outside army which carries out the aggression. I think the Reagan administration is now in a position where it has to increase the military pressure against Nicaragua, but the American population is still resisting these steps, a fact that is reflected to some limited extent in Congress.

HD: Is there any way constitutionally to stop Reagan from intervening?

NC: Oh yes, there is a way to constitutionally stop Reagan. Congress can cut off the funds and if there is sufficient popular pressure, Congress will. Congress reflects, to some extent, popular pressure and, in fact, there is a lot of opposition to direct intervention in Nicaragua and El Salvador. For example, in the first months of the Reagan administration in early 1981, when the White Paper[5] came out and they were trying to lay the groundwork for direct military intervention in El Salvador and Nicaragua, there was enormous popular opposition in the country; there were demonstrations, letters to the White House etc. In fact, some polls indicate that up to 50 percent of the population would be willing to support direct resistance if American military forces were sent. This is far beyond anything that was true during the Vietnam War. So there is a lot of popular opposition and Congress reflects that.

On the other hand, the congressional opposition is very weak, because in a certain sense it has no moral basis. That is one of the reasons it always ultimately fails. Most of the congressional opposition basically accepts the fundamental assumptions of the Reagan administration. There is very little difference in the assumptions.

HD: What are these assumptions?

NC: The assumptions are that the United States has a perfect right to use force and violence to achieve its ends anywhere in the world. Anyone who refuses to obey American wishes and orders is by definition a "communist," and it is therefore legitimate to destroy them in "self-defense."

HD: And those assumptions are shared by the military?

NC: They are shared by just about everybody. Well, I don't know if they are shared by the population, but they are certainly shared by the political classes: by the articulate intelligentsia, the corporate elite that runs the country and the military-bureaucratic components of the national security state system — what you may roughly call the "political classes." They share the assumption that the United States is global judge and executioner. We have a moral duty to use violence to attain our ends anywhere.

HD: So that has not changed since the end of World War II?

NC: No, that has never changed and, in fact, that could not change. There is no change among the elites. Some minor changes in a few individuals, no doubt, but basically that understanding is accepted. The only questions are, "can we get away with it?" or "is it tactically advisable?" or "would it be too costly?" Or sometimes there is the question of whether it would be too bloody; so there are some people who would draw the line at some point, say, napalm attacks that kill too many children. That would be too much. But a smaller amount would be okay, and so on and so forth.

Of course, it's never put that way. The way it's put is that we have a right to stop Russian-supported aggression anywhere in the world. Anything we do in the world is a defensive act to stop the Russians. It doesn't matter if the Russians aren't there, it is still a defensive act to stop the Russians. So, in this respect, you could compare the American propaganda system to Hitler's propaganda system — Hitler was simply defending Germany against the Jewish and Bolshevik threat. Or, you can compare it to the Russian propaganda system. When the Russians invaded Czechoslovakia and Afghanistan, they said they were doing it to defend themselves against American and West German militarism. That's the way great powers work.

In a well-indoctrinated society with very effective systems of thought control, people actually believe this kind of nonsense. The United States is one of the most indoctrinated societies in the world and consequently this ridiculous nonsense is believed. For example, when the United States invaded Grenada, people literally discussed the claim that Grenada was a military threat to the United States. And it was discussed as if this were a serious allegation, not mere black comedy. And right now, for example, there is talk about the Russian-sponsored aggression in Nicaragua and El Salvador. That the Russians aren't there is irrelevant, because this is theology, not rational discourse. In theology facts are irrelevant. This theological system is accepted by the political classes virtually without exception, though they do argue a little bit — maybe the Russian threat has been exaggerated. The fact that we are considering American aggression and terrorism is almost never understood.

Returning to Vietnam, exactly the same is true. You may have seen an article in the *New York Times* a couple of days ago, where Walter Mondale and Gary Hart were trying to determine their differences with regard to Vietnam. Mondale, for example, said that until 1969, he accepted the idea that there was Russian-sponsored aggression in Vietnam. But after 1969, he found out that this was exaggerated. Well, that's like talking to a madman. To say there was Russian-sponsored aggression in a country that we were attacking when there weren't any Russians — that is essentially the talk of a madman.

The American government at that time concocted the concept of "internal aggression." Adlai Stevenson[6] at the United Nations, and others, said we were fighting "internal aggression" in Vietnam, meaning: aggression by the Vietnamese against us. That's "internal aggression." In fact, Reagan advisers have noted the common thread connecting Greece in the late 1940s, Vietnam in the early 1960s and Central America today. They say, "Yes, all these cases involve fighting internal aggression," meaning aggression by some population in its own country against Americans who are invading. That's defending us, and defending them, against internal aggression.

This is a level of thought control which is very difficult to imagine, but one has to recognize that dealing with the United States is like dealing with Khomeini's Iran, a country that is in the grip of a fanatic delusional system. Reagan undoubtedly believes that if we bomb Nicaragua, or if American pilots engage in reconnaissance flights to help the Salvadoran Air Force bomb civilians, that it is defense. It's defense of the Salvadorans against the Russians.

Now the question is whether that can be sold to the population. There's quite a split between the attitudes of the population as a whole and the attitudes of the articulate political classes. You can see this in the polls with regard to the Vietnam War. The Gallup Poll organization reviews attitudes every year. Every year, they ask the question: "Do you think that the Vietnam War was a mistake or was it fundamentally and morally wrong?" In 1982, among the population as a whole, the percentage that said it was fundamentally and morally wrong and not just a mistake was 72 percent. Among the people they call "opinion leaders," which includes clergy and so on, it was about 40 percent. And among the articulate intelligentsia it would probably be close to zero.

That brings us back to the original point. The question is

whether these attitudes will affect Congress, which represents the political classes? Their opposition to American aggression is undermined by the fact that they regard it as fundamentally legitimate. So their opposition is basically tactical. "Will it cost us too much?" or "will it work?" or maybe it's "too bloody." And that means that in a real conflict they appear to the public as immoral and cowardly, because after all, if the actions we are taking are legitimate, if it is legitimate to use military force to defend the Salvadorans by killing them in El Salvador, then why are these cowards saying we shouldn't do it?

Take a look at the *New Republic*, just the other day. The *New Republic* is as close as one can find to an official journal of American liberalism. They had an editorial statement on El Salvador in which they stated that we must continue to give military aid to the government of El Salvador "regardless of how many are murdered." And then it went on to say that if the choice for the people of El Salvador is between communism and war, then the American people will choose war. That is legitimate, because the American people have a right to choose for the Salvadoran people since we are the agents of divine authorities. So we have a right to choose between communism and war for the people of El Salvador — and we choose war. And then it went on to say that if aid to the counter-revolutionaries fails, we'll have to move in directly. But then, since this is a liberal journal, it says "well of course we're doing this in defense of human rights." So, if we intervene in El Salvador, it will be against the death squads, as our history in Central America shows very clearly. And then it says, the reason why we must give military aid, regardless of how many people are murdered there, is because we are protecting them from a worse evil: communism. Now, those stupid peasants may not understand that, so we will have to kill them all — in the interest of defending human rights.

This *New Republic* editorial evokes no comment in the liberal mainstream. The same left-liberal writers continue to contribute and raise no objections. That's essentially the liberal view. And the spectrum goes from the liberal view, which says we have to kill as many of them as is necessary to save them from the worst evil, over to the hawkish views, which don't even raise the questions. That's roughly the spectrum of opinion in the political classes.

HD: That reminds me of Franco's statement that if it was necessary to kill one million Spaniards in order to save Spain from communism, he would do that.

NC: The only difference is that the *New Republic* goes way beyond Franco, because they don't say that it is necessary to kill a million people in El Salvador. They say you may have to kill all of them. They say, "regardless of how many are murdered" we still have to do it, in order to save them from communism. So that is a step beyond the standard fascist argument.

HD: So you think that the political establishment simply cannot learn?

NC: Well, *learning* is not really the point. I mean, they learn a lot, they learn what is important to them: how to do it better next time. But apart from that, there is nothing to learn. We were right to attack Vietnam, so there is nothing to learn except why we failed and how to do it better next time.

They don't regard American intervention or aggression as wrong. How could it be wrong? Since we are by definition perfect and everything we do is, by definition, in the interest of human rights, what can we learn except how to improve our tactics? This goes way back in U.S. history. Incidentally, so does the appeal to the Bolshevik threat. I think the first use of this appeal in the context of Central America was in the late 1920s, when President Calvin Coolidge sent the marines to Nicaragua in an intervention that led to the establishment of Somoza and the killing of Sandino [leader of anti-U.S. imperialist movement in Nicaragua]. The justification that was offered by the government at that time was that we had to block Mexico, because Mexico was the proxy of the Bolsheviks. So we were blocking Russian-backed aggression. Right now we are stopping Russian aggression, carried out by its proxy Cuba.

But in fact, if you go back earlier, before they began to use that argument, we were carrying out interventions in the Philippines, Haiti, the Dominican Republic and so on, where, of course, we represented civilization and progress. But those people were just too backward to understand this, so therefore for their own good we'd have to invade them, and so on.

This goes way back to the "Indian Wars." There is a straight line all the way back in American history to the earliest days. The attack on the indigenous population, as the country was conquered, was genocidal. People don't realize that. That's celebrated in the United States. It's not regarded as anything wrong. I'll give you an example. I live in an upper-middle class town, which is progressive, lots of liberal Democrats, educated, professional, very good schools and so on. In 1969 I had a daughter in school — the date is important because this was right after the My Lai massacre. She was in fourth grade at that time and she was reading a book called *Exploring New England*, a book about the glorious colonial past. I happened to look through it once. The book was structured around a 10-year-old boy, Robert, who was being taken through colonial history by some older man. They got to the point of the Pequot Indian massacre, right here in this area, a massacre where the colonists simply attacked a peaceful village, burned it down and killed every man, woman and child — about 600 people. This was done to great applause at the time.

Well, how was it recorded? The book went through the massacre, described it accurately, and then at the end the boy, Robert, turned to the older man and said: "I wish I had been a man and had been there." That is, the whole description is positive. This was one of the glories of our colonial past. And as you go through American history, it was the same.

Now, when the United States attacked the Philippines — a brutal attack in which several hundred thousand people were murdered and tortured, with extensive destruction, villages burned down and so on — the attack was carried out by the same soldiers who had fought the native Americans. The top military command got their training in the "Indian Wars." And this was accepted at home. There was a small critical group, but in general it was accepted. We have to do this, they said, because right now the Filipinos have to be crushed in their own interest. They will ultimately see that we have benevolent intentions and since they don't understand that, we have to kill them and torture them and burn down their villages and kill their children and so on and so forth. And that strain runs all the way through American history, right up to the present. That is what is called "American idealism" or "American moralism" by many historians.

There has barely been a change among the political classes. Of course, there were changes among the American population and their perception of these things. But that does not affect the understanding of the elite groups. If they changed their conceptions, they wouldn't be able to do these things. They'd have to drop out and they'd be replaced by someone else. It's just like asking whether the board of managers of General Motors could learn not to maximize profits. If someone learns not to maximize profits, he is no longer on the board of directors, because that's the nature of the institution. The nature of the institution is to maximize profits, the nature of the

American state is to maximize global control in the interests of the dominant domestic groups. If somebody doesn't accept these assumptions, they can't be part of the system.

HD: Could we say, then, that the United States is an imperialist system in the Leninist sense, with the multinational corporations' interests as the driving element and the state as the executing element?

NC: We know what the driving interests are, because the United States is a very open society, probably the most open society in the world and one of the freest in the world, and one result is that we have a lot of documentary evidence about the United States. So we have the documents, we know what the planners were thinking.

If you go back to World War II, probably the most dovish, moderate, liberal, peace-oriented figure in the diplomacy of the period was George Kennan, who is now a scholar. In the late 1940s he was the head of the Policy Planning Staff of the State Department. He published a series of very revealing papers which were written by the State Department's planning staff. This is the dovish side, the liberal side. He wrote one study, "PPS 23," specifically directed to Asia, but it was similar elsewhere in the world. It says that since the United States has six percent of the world's population and uses 50 percent of the world's resources, and given that this disparity causes opposition in other parts of the world, we must construct our policies to ensure that this disparity is maintained.

So our fundamental policy commitment is to ensure that we will use 50 percent of the world's resources with our six percent of the world's population. And, he says, we're going to have to be realistic about this. We must put aside any sentimental concerns about human rights and democracy, in Asia and anywhere, and we have to be ready to use harsh measures. And, in fact, he had similar conceptions with regard to Latin America. Around 1950, Kennan was asked to give a lecture to the Latin American ambassadors and he explained to them that the United States would have to support Latin American states that use violence against their own populations. He said that there is nothing immoral about this because the communists are traitors and therefore, if the state uses force and violence to attack the communists, there is nothing wrong with that. And this is the standard American position. John F. Kennedy, for example, stated in the early 1960s that governments of the civil-military type are the kind that are appropriate for El

Salvador. And that's why there is such overwhelming support when the United States uses force against democratic regimes.

Take a look at Guatemala. The 1954 coup against Arbenz[7] was supported without noticeable dissent. But more interesting, in a way, is what happened in 1963. In 1963 it looked as though Arévalo[8] would run for office again and, of course, everybody believed that he would win. So the Kennedy administration, which was liberal, intervened to support a military coup to prevent the elections from taking place, because they were afraid that this "communist" — somebody who would not follow American orders — would win in Guatemala. And that pattern is followed throughout.

Take, for example, the Dominican Republic. That is a more subtle case. In the early 1960s, after Trujillo[9] was assassinated, there was a brief democratic period. Juan Bosch was elected with popular support. He was a mild social democrat, not a revolutionary, like a liberal Democrat in the United States. Well, in order for him to maintain his position, he was going to have to develop support in popular organizations that would stand up against the military forces, which of course were the main threat. The military forces were created and sponsored by the United States. Now, how do you create popular support? The only way to do it is by carrying out agrarian reforms and supporting the labor unions, in short, mild reformist efforts to build up the popular support which conceivably could be a counterweight to the military, to block a military coup. Well, the Kennedy administration refused to back him. Of course, the American embassy is the most important power bloc in any of these countries and Ambassador John Bartlow Martin, who was a Kennedy appointment, refused to support any such actions and, in fact, strongly opposed any activities that would help to build the popular support that could be a counterweight to the military. So they opposed the agrarian reform, they opposed various measures that would allow unions to develop, they also strongly opposed contacts with Europe, and so on and so forth. Now, that is the more subtle approach. When these popular organizations do develop, as they developed in El Salvador in the 1970s, we have to move in with direct violence and destroy them.

All of this goes way back. I think it was Thomas Jefferson who said that the United States has a hemisphere all to itself. By World War II, it was not just the hemisphere, it was a substantial part of the world. From 1939 to 1945 the State Department and the Council on Foreign Relations carried out an extensive series of studies concerning the shape of the post-war world. This was called the "War–Peace Studies Program." It ran from 1939 to 1945 and involved the top planners of the State Department and the Council on Foreign Relations, which essentially is the business input into foreign policy.

Those studies are very interesting. They are never investigated by academic scholarship. They're public, but they might just as well be censored. They are never discussed, there's never an article written about them in the mainstream literature. The reasons are plain if you look at their content — they reveal very rational imperial planning, no sentimentality. They constructed the concept of what they called the "grand area." The "grand area" was to be a region "strategically necessary for world control," in their words. That's the grand area and the grand area had to be coordinated with and subordinated to the needs of the American economy. Then they went through a geo-political analysis to figure out what the grand area should be and the conclusion was that at a minimum it should include the Western hemisphere, the Far East and the former British Empire. The maximum would be the universe. And then they developed institutional planning concerning the grand area, that is, how it should be reorganized and subordinated to the needs of the American economy. Then plans were made for South East Asia and so on and so forth.

Well, that's rational imperial planning. Of course, there's a commitment by scholarship and the media to ensure that this picture isn't presented. What is presented is a picture of benevolent, endearing, good-hearted people, who sometimes don't understand, which is why they make mistakes.

So, in the Vietnam War it was accepted across the entire spectrum that the intentions of the executive branch were benign. Take, for example, John K. Fairbank, who was one of the leading Asian scholars and liberals, so far to the left that he was one of the targets of McCarthyism. He was a Harvard professor and President of the American Historical Society. In December 1968, the year of the Tet offensive, he gave his presidential address to the American Historical Society in which he said that the Vietnam War was a disaster, but that we had entered it in "an excess of righteousness and disinterested benevolence." Now, that's the critique from the extreme left of mainstream scholarship. We entered the war in an excess of righteousness and disinterested benevolence. That's Vietnam, in the year of the Tet offensive, when this country was blowing up and even businessmen had turned against the war. But, that's what you were hearing from a left-liberal Harvard professor.

The United States is a very interesting country in this respect. There is great deal of freedom and nobody is forcing scholarship and the media to conform to the party line. Nevertheless, the degree of subordination to what should properly be called the party line is comparable to a totalitarian state.

Returning to Central America. I think it's the way this internal struggle between the different forces in the United States ends up that is going to determine whether the United States intervenes directly in Central America or not. The congressional opposition is weak, because it has no moral basis. If Reagan brings the issue to the public, there is a very small basis for the congressional opposition, because he is going to say: "Look, these guys are cowards. They agree that we have to stop communism. They agree that we have to stop Russian aggression in El Salvador, but they don't want to do anything, because they are cowards." And what is the answer? The answer obviously will be: "Yep, they are cowards."

HD: Will the population buy this?

NC: Maybe the population will have good enough sense not to pay attention to any of this stuff. But in so far as there is a debate, the opposition is on very weak ground.

HD: Is it possible that Reagan thinks he might lose and therefore will intervene before the elections, in order to ensure that the Democrats cannot "sell out Central America" if they come to power?

NC: I think the chances are not very great. Sending American troops would be very unpopular. Because, despite what the political classes may feel, the population is strongly opposed to it, very strongly opposed to it. They will accept it in places like Grenada, where it is a cheap victory. In fact, the Grenada victory evoked lots of jingoist sentiments, which are very reminiscent of the 1930s when Hitler became the most popular leader in history through his own cheap victories. That's what the mood was like here during Grenada. This was a glorious victory with 6000 American elite troops overcoming the resistance of 40 Cubans and a few dozen Grenadan military men. And then these 6000 elite troops were given 8000 medals for valor to celebrate this enormous accomplishment. When the 82nd Airborne Brigade came back, they were treated as combat heroes.

You can sort of understand it on the part of the population, because what they were being told was that Grenada was posing a military threat to the United States. Now, the very fact that those words were pronounced indicates how well people have been brainwashed in this country. The example of Khomeini is really appropriate. The very fact that people could hear the former Chairman of the Joint Chiefs of Staff on the radio publicly saying that Grenada is a military threat to the United States, without just exploding into raucous laughter, is an indication of the degree of indoctrination.

Such victories lead to jingoist sentiments, if they are cheap. But in Central America, it's not going to be cheap. There is a principled opposition among the public and large sectors of the population recognize that if the United States intervenes in Central America, it is going to be pretty violent. Well, that doesn't always find its way into the mainstream mass media, but it is there.

HD: So do you think that unless there is a dramatic deterioration in the situation in El Salvador, Reagan will not intervene before the elections?

NC: I think they will try to keep things on hold in Nicaragua and El Salvador.

HD: And after the election?

NC: After the election they have three years to intervene directly. But I don't know. They have to calculate the costs. One of the costs they have to calculate is domestic disruption. They want a passive, obedient society. They are frightened by what happened in the 1960s.

There was a very interesting, and very frank, study done in 1975 by the Trilateral Commission, which is basically the liberal wing of the international capitalist elite, including Japan, Western Europe and the United States. The study is called *The Crisis of Democracy*. The "crisis of democracy" was that large parts of the population became politically active. They became mobilized for action through a variety of groupings and entered the political arena. That's intolerable, because the way democracy is supposed to work is that the privileged elites run the show completely and the population is supposed to be passive and obedient. Their concept of democracy is rather like the feudal system: there is a nobility which is benevolent and there are commoners who are allowed to make requests. And since the nobility is so benevolent, it will occasionally accede to their requests. But if the commoners begin asking for too much, then the answer is "no," because of course privilege cannot be challenged.

This kind of crisis was taking place in American society during the 1960s. That crisis had to be overcome, the population had to be restored to apathy and passivity. I think they *are* learning from history. After the Vietnam War, a major battle was undertaken to bring back this passivity and they want to make sure it doesn't happen again. Thus, I think the mood and actions of the population would be a major factor when escalation is considered.

HD: Do you think that international opinion is secondary?

NC: I think American elites are smart enough to realize that most of their allies are just colonies. Britain, for example, is almost totally colonized. Some noises may be made by some of the neighboring countries, but they can't do anything. Their position is far too weak.

HD: So the principal factor would be the internal costs?

NC: Yes, the internal costs plus the actual material costs.

HD: It is evident that Reagan has been breaking several U.S. and international laws since 1981. It is, therefore, the duty of members of Congress to impeach him. Why hasn't that happened?

NC: Again, by definition, international law does not apply to the United States. People in power are not subject to law. The law is something to be used against people who are powerless. That's the nature of the law, particularly international law.

It's not just Reagan. Take, for example, President Kennedy. When Kennedy sent the American Air Force to attack South Vietnam, he violated international and domestic law. The United States is a signatory to the UN Charter and the UN Charter makes it a crime, in fact a war crime, to use force in international affairs. There is only one exception: you may defend yourself against armed attack. And that's what the U.S. government appeals to while arming the Contras to attack Nicaragua and mining the harbors in Nicaragua. That is supposed to be self-defense against armed attack. The reason they use this wording is that otherwise the actions are illegal, illegal under international law and also under American law — the UN Charter is a fully recognized treaty and therefore is, under the U.S. Constitution, part of the "supreme law of the land."

So, Kennedy and Eisenhower and most of the rest have always been in flagrant violation of the supreme law of the land, because they have repeatedly used force and violence in international affairs. And this is not a minor misdemeanor. It's not something like Watergate. This is serious. In fact, this is what we hanged people for at Nuremberg. The legal system that emerged from World War II regarded this as the major crime. Other crimes were secondary; the major crime was the crime of aggression, the use of force in international affairs. Of course, that is never taken seriously by the United States or any other country. How could it be? This is the kind of principle you use against enemies.

HD: If you read the transcripts of Reagan's interviews, it's obvious that he is incapable of formulating a coherent argument. How can somebody like him be the head of a complex social and state system? What function does he perform for the dominant classes? Why is he there?

NC: He serves several functions and he is there because of his talents as what they call the "great communicator." He produces a stream of nonsense that is ridiculous and embarrassing, but there are powerful groups which stand behind him, whose interests he represents and serves.

Presidents are generally figures who are sold to the population by groups of investors who have decided that they have an interest in taking over state power. They put forth an individual who they think will enable their investment to pay off if he is elected. That's why presidential campaigns are a kind of Hollywood show. The point is to sell a candidate, to get the voters to choose one or another group of investors. It's sometimes even called "selling the President."

So what Reagan says is of use only in so far as it can be effective in controlling the population. If he looks appealing, smiles and all these other things, that's all that counts.

HD: And he is still serving that purpose?

NC: He is serving that purpose quite well. In fact, it looks as if he is going to be reelected.

3

The United States: The Superpower That is Afraid of Small Countries

There is at the head of this great continent a very powerful country, very rich, very warlike, and capable of anything.

Simón Bolívar[1]

... the United States seems destined to plague and torment the continent in the name of freedom.

Simón Bolívar[2]

Economic nationalism is the common denominator of the new aspirations for industrialization. Latin Americans are convinced that the first beneficiaries of the development of a country's resources should be the people of that country.

Laurence Duggan, U.S. State Department[3]

... the principal actions to be undertaken were paramilitary which hopefully would provoke cross-border attacks by Nicaraguan forces and thus serve to demonstrate Nicaragua's aggressive nature and possibly call into play the Organization of American States' provisions. It was hoped that the Nicaraguan Government would clamp down on civil liberties demonstrating its allegedly inherent totalitarian nature and thus increase domestic dissent within the country.

D. MacMichael, former CIA analyst, testifying at World Court[4]

---

* This interview was conducted in May 1985.

Heinz Dieterich: President Reagan justified his trade embargo against Nicaragua saying that the "policies and actions of Nicaragua constitute an unusual and extraordinary threat to the national security and foreign policy of the United States" and he therefore declared a national emergency "to deal with that threat." How can an underdeveloped peasant nation of three million people constitute an "extraordinary threat" to the security of the United States?

Noam Chomsky: The threat to the security of the United States is too ludicrous to discuss, but the threat to U.S. foreign policy is quite real. In fact, in a certain sense it is the small, weak countries that pose the greatest threat to American foreign policy. It is quite remarkable to see the extraordinary savagery that the United States has displayed against the weakest and most inconsequential countries, for example Laos and Grenada. The weaker the country, the greater the savagery. Nicaragua is a case in point.

It makes a lot of sense when you think about the basis on which American policy is formulated. The fundamental principles of American foreign policy, as they were articulated quite clearly in the 1940s, are designed to ensure what George Kennan once called "the protection of our raw materials." He was referring to Latin America and he went on to explain against whom we are protecting "our raw materials." Well, supposedly against the Russians, but that is only to frighten the domestic population; in fact, we are protecting "our raw materials" primarily from the indigenous population. The problem is that the indigenous populations often have the tendency to try to use "our raw materials" for their own purposes. Now, that's a conspiracy that has to be stopped. Why are little countries like Laos and Grenada and Nicaragua so significant? Well, the reason is — and this has always been well understood in American foreign policy — that these countries may show some concern for the welfare of their own populations. And if that turns out to be in any sense successful, if there is successful economic and social development, it may constitute a model for other places. It will have a demonstration effect.

It is interesting the way planners talk about this, the way Kissinger talked about it, for example, in the case of Chile under Allende. He said that the example of Chile might infect other countries — it would be a virus. It's a disease, in other words. Successful development is a disease that might infect other countries. Another image that the planners like to use is that of a rotten apple. There is one rotten apple in the barrel and it may infect the whole barrel. The "rot" that they are concerned with is the "rot" of successful economic and social development, which may infect others nearby and which has to be stopped.

The smaller and more insignificant the country, the more dangerous the threat. And you can easily see why. Take, for example, Laos. The United States employed extraordinary savagery to block democracy in Laos. We overthrew the only democratic government they had ever had and installed an extreme right-wing dictatorship in 1958. Later we started bombing the country; we ended up subjecting it to one of the most savage bombings in history. Laos is a society of isolated peasant villages, where most of the people who lived there didn't even know there was an outside world until those things appeared up there in the sky and started dropping bombs on them.

Why did we have to destroy the peasant society of Laos? Well, they were carrying out a low-level agrarian revolution run by the Pathet Lao, which was also beginning to introduce health and educational measures and some sort of national integration, and that had to be stopped. The point is that a revolution in a place like Laos is particularly dangerous, because if the people of Thailand, who are in fact ethnically related, see successful development in a place as weak and insignificant as Laos, then they will ask the obvious question: Why not here, in a richer and better placed society?

The same is true of Grenada. The United States has no interest in Grenada. They wouldn't know if Grenada disappeared from the face of the earth. But as soon as Maurice Bishop's government came into power [in 1979], the United States immediately demonstrated extraordinary hostility. They cut off aid, they ran threatening military operations, they did everything to make sure that the pressure would crack them. Why is Grenada so significant? Well, if the measures undertaken by the Bishop government could have succeeded in Grenada, then in other countries nearby the question would obviously have been asked: Why not us?

The weaker the country, the greater the threat — because the greater the adversity under which the success is reached, the more significant the result. Therefore, we had this consistent exhibition of quite extreme savagery and violence directed against tiny and insignificant countries that could be a source of infection, that could be "rotten apples" that would infect the barrel.

Now, turning to Nicaragua. As soon as anyone looked at the earliest Sandinista programs, it was obvious that this was going to be an enemy that had to be destroyed. The earliest programs of the Sandinistas were educational programs which enormously increased literacy, health programs which reduced infant mortality and increased life expectancy — in fact, they won an award from the World Health Organization for achievements in this field — and an agrarian reform program that actually worked. Well, that means that they are beginning to steal "our resources." They are using "our" resources for their own purposes. They are threatening to carry out independent social and economic and national development outside the framework of American domination and control. And that means that they are posing a threat to the whole international system dominated by the United States, in which "our" resources are available and the areas are subordinated to the needs of the people who at home run the American economy. That has to be stopped. This has always been very explicit in American foreign policy.

For example, in the George Kennan speech that I mentioned, which he gave at a secret briefing for Latin American ambassadors, he said that one major concern of American foreign policy was the protection of "our resources" and that we must not be hesitant about supporting harsh repression by the local governments. He also said that it's better to support a harsh government than a liberal government which will tolerate communists. What he meant by "communists" and what the term means in American political rhetoric is anyone who is concerned for the welfare of their own population instead of our welfare, which is obviously the transcendent value. And we tried to drive these people into becoming Soviet satellites. This is consistent all the way back.

HD: U.S. Secretary of State Shultz said that he did not expect the embargo "to have much impact on the Nicaraguan economy." If that is the case, why did they declare the embargo?

NC: It will have an impact in two respects. It will cause greater suffering in Nicaragua, which is very important, and it will force Nicaragua into the hands of the Soviet Union, which is also very important. You have noticed that the United States does this consistently, with any region, and with any country that begins to escape our control. If we can't destroy it by, say, invasion or subversion, we try to drive it into the hands of the Russians, because that then provides a justification for the attack that we must carry out against it for other reasons. We have to prevent independent development. That's why we have to attack. Therefore, we need an excuse; the only excuse is that it is a Russian base, therefore we have to make it a Russian base. This is done with complete consistency.

In Guatemala, for example, we did that to the Arévalo government and then the Arbenz government, which were democratic governments, capitalist governments with essentially New Deal style programs. When they began to fall under that same heresy of using their resources for their own purposes, carrying out some independent development concerned with the domestic population, the United States claimed that they had to be overthrown. It's hard to justify attacking a capitalist democratic government, so the United States did everything it could to drive them into the hands of the Russians, threatening them, refusing to send them arms. The United States literally sent bombers armed with nuclear weapons to Nicaragua to show their resolve in the assault against Guatemala. The fanatic extent to which they were willing to go to undermine this capitalist democracy that was going the wrong way is astonishing if you think about it. Finally, we forced them to the point where they asked for some arms from the Eastern Bloc and that provided the justification for the attack.

The first "good" effect of the embargo is that it increases suffering and, therefore, we are probably increasing internal dissidence. And the second "good" effect is that it will drive them into the hands of the Russians, providing the justification which is required for the attack that the United States intends to, in fact, does carry out against them anyway. Third, it has a "good" effect in the United States. It remains to be seen, but they hope that the effect will be to create a situation of confrontation and therefore to evoke the mood of chauvinist fanaticism that many governments attempt to elicit in their own population when they are trying to arouse them for attack against some hated enemy. And, what they are hoping for, I am sure, is that the Russians will send ships, which can then be blocked by the American navy so they will have a nice confrontation and people will get more hysterical than they are, and so on and so forth. That's the way you have to work if you are trying to destroy a really dangerous enemy — like a tiny country that is beginning to steal "our resources" for its own purposes.

HD: Is it foreseeable that there will be a military intervention further down the road?

NC: I doubt it — I think we are being a little bit misled here. Let me draw an analogy with the 1960s, since we have a very close analogy to what was happening then in Vietnam. In the 1960s, the United States was attacking South Vietnam and that attack was very severe. In fact, it had begun in the 1950s. By 1965, the resistance in South Vietnam had reached a point where the United States had to start a land invasion. They had bombed South Vietnam for several years, but they had to actually send troops to invade South Vietnam on the ground.

Meanwhile, the bombing of South Vietnam that had been going on for years was stepped up extensively in February 1965. It was far more severe and, in general, throughout the entire war, the main burden of the attack was against the South. Yet the protests that happened both in the United States and Europe were primarily over the bombing of North Vietnam. The American attack against South Vietnam passed with very limited protest. The Pentagon itself recognized this. Secretary McNamara, who was Secretary of Defense at the time, made secret statements that were later revealed in the Pentagon Papers in which he pointed out that both in the United States and Europe the main protest was against the bombing of the North, not the much more severe bombing of the South. And the reason is plain. The bombing of North Vietnam carried with it the threat of international complications — that's pretty harmful to the United States or Europe, since it could lead to world war. So, there was concern. But in the case of South Vietnam, where it was simply a matter of massacring peasants, there were no international complications. It caused, therefore, very little protest.

Now, let's come to today. It's really very similar. The United States has been engaged for several years in a massive, savage attack against El Salvador and that has been stepped up recently. There is now extensive bombing of El Salvador. There are huge free-fire zones, bombing coordinated by American military planes flying from sanctuaries in Honduras and Panama. That's all been stepped up. It's a huge massacre that has been going on for a long time and is continuing with very little protest over it.

On the other hand, as part of the periphery of the attack against El Salvador, we are also attacking Nicaragua. That has caused protest, because it could lead to international complications. Now, the analogy to the 1960s is rather close, with El Salvador being like South Vietnam and Nicaragua being like North Vietnam. In both cases, the general motive is the same: to ensure that none of these places can extricate themselves from subordination to the American-run global system. But the main brunt of the attack is now against El Salvador, just as the main brunt of the attack in the 1960s was against South Vietnam.

The protest was over the attack on North Vietnam and is over the attack on Nicaragua at the moment, because of the international complications associated with it. So I doubt very much that we will invade Nicaragua, just as I never expected that we would invade North Vietnam. What we will try to do is prevent any successful development there and meanwhile crush the popular movement in the countries that are our primary concern. We had to destroy South Vietnam in the early 1960s and we did. The United States won that war. And it is now committed to trying to crush any sort of popular organization in El Salvador and I suspect that we will win that war.

The press, incidentally, is barely reporting. There is some reporting about the Contras' atrocities and also about Nicaragua. But there is virtually no report about the much greater atrocities being conducted by the United States and its client army in El Salvador. That's barely discussed. For example, when was the last time you saw a reporter who went to the refugee camps in Honduras to interview people about what's going on in El Salvador and the American bombing?

HD: As one official stated recently, the dilemma for the U.S. administration is that they don't want another Cuba but neither do they want another Vietnam. So, what can they do?

NC: They can do what the United States has done successfully throughout most of its history. The whole history of the United States in Latin America is one of destroying popular movements or crushing any move to independence and installing brutal and vicious dictatorships by which they keep the region under control. That's the primary reason why it is one of the real horror chambers of the modern world. This has been going on for over a century. The United States attacked Nicaragua in 1854; 131 years ago the U.S. Navy destroyed a town in Nicaragua, San Juan del Norte. They bombarded it and burned it down because there was an alleged insult to an American millionaire. In this century, the United States has invaded Cuba, Panama, Mexico, Haiti, the Dominican Republic, Guatemala, Nicaragua; every place where we have been, every place of intervention, the result is almost invariably the same. So it has nothing to do with the Russians. For example, Wilson sent American troops to the Dominican Republic and Haiti, besides

invading Mexico, before the Bolshevik revolution. The pretence
then was that we were defending ourselves against the Germans.
They were around as much as the Russians are around in Nicaragua
today.

The results of these interventions — or, rather, brutal and
murderous counterinsurgency wars — were that in Haiti the United
States succeeded in reinstating slavery, torturing and burning
villages. They left the Duvalier dictatorship, which has been kept in
power since and has converted the country into undoubtedly one of
the most miserable parts of the world. In Nicaragua, after most of it
had been under Marine occupation, we left the Somoza dictatorship
in power. In Guatemala, the United States overthrew the democratic
government and left a series of Guatemalan Himmlers in power.

In the Dominican Republic, the counterinsurgency under Wilson
and Harding came first, ending up with the Trujillo dictatorship.
That lasted until 1960. Then there was a brief period of democracy
when the Bosch government came in. Everyone knew there was
going to be a military coup sooner or later — unless Bosch was able
to build up popular support to combat it. The only way he could
have built up popular support was by measures like agrarian reform, labor organizing, and so on. The American embassy under
Kennedy refused to allow him to do those things and there was a
military coup which was supported by the United States. And then,
in 1965, when there was again a threat of Dominican democracy, the
United States just sent in the Marines and installed another brutal
dictatorship. Finally, after the whole country was demoralized and
crushed and sold out to corporations, they were willing to allow
what they call "elections." Now, that is the typical history of the
United States in Latin America. This is just another phase, it's nothing new. Everything that's happening now has happened a dozen
times before.

HD: Why is it impossible for Latin American nations to be
sovereign and live free from interference by the United States?

NC: Well, it's impossible because they can't live in the shadow of a
violent and sadistic superpower that is committed to domination
and control. The United States is committed to ensuring that the
resources of Latin America are available for the American economy
in the manner in which the American economy desires them. This is
part of a global pattern, but of course, the imprint is heaviest on the
Caribbean Basin, where the influence of American power has been
greatest for the longest period.

If we ask ourselves why the United States is so fussed about Cuba, the answer is the same. The answer is given very clearly by some simple statistics. For example, there was recently a study by the Overseas Development Council, which puts out a "quality of life index" every year compiled on the basis of mortality rate, infant mortality, life expectancy, and literacy. This is for the world. I think the top countries are places like Iceland and Japan, then you go down to the Scandinavian countries and then you get to the United States, which had a rating of 97 in their index. And Canada is about the same, a little higher. The next country in Latin America is Cuba: 95. Then you have to go down to 89 before you start reaching the rich Latin American countries. Well, any country that is that high on the quality of life index — that is, highest in its achievements in health standards, reducing infant mortality, increasing life expectancy, increasing literacy — obviously that country is an enemy. I mean, it must be that they are using their resources for their purposes, not for our purposes. And therefore we are going to destroy them.

In the case of Cuba, the United States has done everything it can to drive them into the hands of the Russians — to ensure that there is a maximum amount of internal repression and brutality inside Cuba to reduce the possibility that it could be a model for anyone else. But there is still this tremendously threatening development. While throughout the whole region that the United States supports and backs, you have torture, murder, starvation, slave labor, and so on and so forth, there is one little corner of Latin America that has actually come to match the standard of living of the United States, which is astonishing. This is the richest country in the world, by any possible measure. Cuba is one of the poorest countries in the world and it has approximately the same quality of life index, in terms of health and so on, that the United States has. That's really scary and that's an enemy. That's what they mean when they say, "We can't tolerate another Cuba." It is bad enough that there is one country that can serve as a model for this kind of development. Suppose there were two, suppose there were three.

In fact, back in 1949, State Department Intelligence produced an interesting report in which they warned that there was a dangerous heresy that was spreading over the hemisphere. They said that many people were being influenced by the idea that "governments have a responsibility for the welfare of their population." That's got to be stopped. We can't allow that kind of heresy to go on. Because there is a much deeper responsibility — that is, their responsibility to us.

HD: During the Vietnam protests, you wrote in an essay that resistance to the war may free some of those who participate from the "mind-destroying ideological pressures of American life." Could you explain that a bit?

NC: Well, the United States is an unusual society. It probably has the most class conscious business class of any place in the world. They are organized and intent. You can see it in things like, for example, the development of the public relations industry, which is vastly more advanced in the United States than in any other country. It goes back to the early part of the century and is in fact an organized, business-run propaganda and indoctrination system directed to the mind of the population. Even before World War I, some AT&T executive said that the only threat to the company is the mind of the American people and we have got to control it. They understand this and they work on it. Europe is so far behind us on this that it is not even close. Take a look at, say, lobbying in Congress, or reactionary foundations like the Heritage Foundation[5] that try to control policy and control thought, concentrating on the media, and so on. That's why you can have the phenomenon that in the entire United States there is only one tiny little town that has a socialist mayor. That would be inconceivable in Europe. Or, in the whole American press, I doubt if there is a single journalist who could be called a mild socialist. That would be inconceivable in any other country.

So, on the one hand you have this extremely class conscious ruling class. On the other hand, you have a very low class consciousness among anyone else. There is an enormous disparity. The reasons for it are complicated and go back deep into American history. The result is a very depoliticized society. There is very little engagement in the political process, even if you look at it in the most superficial way. Even things like voting are low. Actual participation is extremely low. You can't be part of a political party. There is no way for individuals to organize in such a way as to, say, put plans forward on the political agenda, unless they come out of relatively privileged sectors, like business. There is almost no other way to do it. It's very hard. One reflection of the depoliticization is the extraordinary religious commitment in the United States, which is far higher than in any other industrial society.

The extent of indoctrination is revealed by the fact that President

Reagan can stand up in public and say that there is a national emergency, a threat to American security from Nicaragua. That is as if Gorbachev got up and said that there is a threat to Russian national security from Luxemburg. I suppose in Russia people would laugh if he said that, but here they don't laugh. There is no protest. That's an example of the extent of indoctrination and control. Well, these are some of the many examples of the "mind destroying ideological pressures of American life."

On the other hand, there are also some positive features that should not be forgotten. One is that the country tends to be quite undisciplined. It's probably the least disciplined country in the world on the part of the population. It has a highly disciplined — in fact, super-disciplined — intellectual class, which is part of the general class consciousness of the privileged. But the lack of class consciousness of most of the population is reflected in a natural dissidence, natural skepticism, unwillingness to obey — there's a kind of superficiality about ideological control. This is one of the reasons why you can have a phenomenon like the American peace movement, which would be difficult to achieve in other countries — spontaneous, unorganized, coming from all corners of the country. That's what is holding back the government right now in Central America.

So it's sort of a mixture. It's a society with a high degree of class consciousness on the part of the privileged, including the educated who are utterly servile, with very few exceptions. On the other hand, the disorganized mass of the population lack any means to develop communication, organization, consciousness, or any kind of critical analysis of society. But they also have a skepticism and general lack of deference to institutional structures. So, it is a complicated mixture.

HD: Could you explain to us a bit why you got involved in the Vietnam War protests and what repercussions that experience had on you?

NC: The real question is: why did I wait so long to get involved? Well, the reasons were obvious. Just look at what is happening in the world; it's frightening to get involved.

HD: Why are there so few intellectuals who get involved?

NC: Because there is a cost. There's a big personal cost. This is a very rich society and it pays people off very well if they conform with the privileged sectors. On the other hand, if you are a traitor to your class — since the state does not have resources of violence to use against the privileged — you don't end up in concentration camps. But life is difficult in many other ways. You are marginalized at school, vilified, ignored and it is just a tremendous burden on your time and energy. For example, if you run on my side of the fence, there is no research assistance and any work to do you do yourself. Because of this great rift between the dissident population and the obedient intellectual, there are enormous demands on those few people who are dissidents. They are under enormous pressure to give talks, to become involved in political organizing, demonstrations and all sorts of things. Well, from a certain point of view these are costs and from another point of view these are privileges, but either way they affect your life.

HD: How would you define your political role and mission in the United States at the moment?

NC: There are certain things that I can do, because of my training, my background and my position. People primarily like me to serve in an educational role. That is, to help counter the deluge of propaganda, the effect of the enormous indoctrination. Very few people are in a position to have the resources, the time, or the training to construct a picture of reality that, in fact, is accurate and runs counter to that of the indoctrination system. There is tremendous demand for that; I mean, I could not give a fraction of the talks that I am asked to give. It would be physically impossible.

HD: With all your outstanding knowledge on these things, how come we never read an article of yours in the *New York Times*?

NC: Well, as I said, the privileged in the United States are highly class conscious and they run a very tight ship. They run a very effective indoctrination system. So, for example, the work of people who don't accept the party line is either ignored, or vilified if it can't be ignored. But they certainly are given no access to the media. Canadian society is very similar to this one, but if I go to Canada I am immediately on the radio and television. The journals review my books and so on and so forth. In the United States that would be virtually impossible. The reason is that this is a class conscious society on the part of the ruling class and they know it is very important not to allow critical, dissident voices to exist, to reach any public. I mean, they have what they call criticism and they carefully nurture it. But if you look carefully, that criticism accepts the basic principles of the party line. So, the kind of criticism that they like is the kind that accepts the party line but says, "You are not doing it too well," or, "You are making a mistake," or something like that. That's fine. The kind of criticism which opposes the party line has to be eliminated. The usual way of eliminating it is to ignore it; when people can't be ignored, they are subjected to abuse, antagonized, etc.

HD: Is linguistics still interesting?

NC: Oh yes, linguistics is fascinating. In fact, the last four or five years have been some of the most exciting years in the history of the field, I think. If it weren't for the outside world, I would spend an awful lot of time on it. It's been a really exciting period.

HD: As a linguist, how do you see the Reagan discourse? Does one need Orwell's *1984* to describe it?

NC: No, you don't need linguistics, you just need elementary common sense. Actually, it goes beyond anything Orwell could imagine, but it's sort of transparent. Any person with any intelligence can only regard it as a comic strip.

HD: In your earlier essays, you quite often used the term "imperialism" or "Western imperialism." For example, you wrote that the Vietnam War was a "manifestation of deeper imperialist forces." But you seem to be more reluctant to use it today. Is this observation correct?

NC: Well, I am not aware of not using it any more. It certainly is the same. We now know more about the careful and thoughtful planning during the 1940s, which went into ensuring that much of the world would be subordinated to the needs of the privileged sectors of the American economic system. And we know a lot more about the measures that have been taken to guarantee these consequences. If that isn't imperialism, then I don't know what it is.

HD: It seems that several U.S. banks laundered drug money and we know from a U.S. Senate investigation that on several occasions the CIA hired Mafia killers to assassinate Cuban President Fidel Castro. What is the relationship between organized crime, the U.S. state and its dominant class?

NC: Well, I'm not an expert on that, but there are things which are obvious. It is perfectly natural for the state to be associated with organized crime. Domestically speaking, organized crime helps control marginal populations, like in the ghettos. For example, if you look at the FBI, which is the national political police, their activities during the 1960s are instructive. They didn't try to destroy black gangs in the ghettos. What they tried to do is kill black organizers in the ghettos. In fact, they even worked together with criminal gangs in the ghettos to try to compel or induce them to kill black organizers in the ghetto. That's typical. The criminal gangs are no threat. They control the ghetto in the interest of outside powers, so they are no problem. But black organizers, like [Black Panther leader] Fred Hampton in Chicago, have to be killed because they are a danger; they might get people to become politicized and to enter the political arena.

The same is true internationally. Take World War II. As the U.S. Army moved up through Italy, it needed somebody to run the place — though it obviously couldn't allow the resistance to run the place. In fact, the resistance had to be dispersed and destroyed. So, primarily, the country was handed back over to the old fascist government. They reinstated the fascist government, but they also revitalized the Mafia, which had been pretty well wiped out by Mussolini. The Mafia was a structure that was available for control in the interests of the conquerors and it was closely related to American crime, which also had been integrated into the American system.

It was also necessary, for example, in the late 1940s to destroy the French labor movement. How do you do that? You need goons, strikebreakers. Who are going to be the strikebreakers? The Mafia, of course. But you need to pay them off. And that's the way the heroin traffic was reconstituted in the late 1940s. And it goes on from there. The criminal elements and the state often have common interests. In fact, the criminal elements and big business are closely integrated. And naturally their common interests often lead them to work together. There are many examples, which shouldn't surprise anybody.

HD: Is it an easy or an uneasy alliance?

NC: It varies, sometimes it's easy and sometimes it's uneasy.

HD: Given the present attacks by the U.S. right wing and the Reagan administration, is the future of the United Nations imperiled?

NC: The Reagan administration is, surely, antagonistic to the United Nations, but I do not think that it will attempt to destroy it, but rather, to discipline it. It should be recognized that hostility to the United Nations has been growing for years, for quite obvious reasons. In the early days, the UN was almost entirely controlled by the United States and, therefore, evoked much enthusiasm here. Over the years, as the UN came to reflect a broader range of global interests, and the power of the United States to coerce declined, antagonism to the UN naturally increased among the educated classes. In the terms favored here, the UN fell under "the tyranny of the majority" — that is, it became marginally more democratic.

In the early days, learned pundits sought to explain why the Russians were always vetoing resolutions (perhaps it was because they raised their children in swaddling clothes, so that they became negative personalities, some proposed). Such inquiries are no longer conducted, now that it is the United States that stands alone on such matters as the Israeli invasion of Lebanon, South Africa, the Law of the Sea, etc. The question that is posed for sober consideration now is not why the USSR is so obstructive, but why the entire world is out of step. The record of commentary on the UN, by the press and intellectuals generally, would be comical if it were not so tragic.

In the Moynihan–Kirkpatrick[6] era, U.S. antagonism towards the United Nations received much more overt expression. Moynihan, in particular, was much lauded for his immense courage in denouncing Idi Amin and standing up against great powers such as Benin — just as Reagan aroused great awe among the faithful for his courage in attacking Grenada [in 1983]. While Moynihan was playing to the local galleries, he was also doing other things. Thus, in his memoirs, he takes credit for preventing the UN from acting to deter the Indonesian invasion of Timor — that is, he takes credit for atrocities at a level that rival Pol Pot (as he is, incidentally, more or less aware). The jokes may amuse his audience of educated Americans, but they are not funny.

The same was true of Kirkpatrick and will remain true. The Reagan administration is a bit beyond the norm in its commitment to violence and terror, and to eliminating any possibility of peaceful settlement of disputes. But it should be recognized that it does not depart greatly from the norm — nor could any U.S. administration take a very different tack given the domestic institutions on which it is, and will be, based.

HD: The United States refused to submit to the jurisdiction of the International Court of Justice (ICJ) in the suit brought against it by Nicaragua for the mining of its harbors. What does this mean for the lawful resolution of international conflicts?

NC: The United States, like other great powers, regards the Rule of Law as a slogan to be used for three purposes: 1) pacifying the domestic population; 2) denouncing official enemies; and 3) dealing with problems where other means prove ineffective, as a last resort. Apart from these concerns, the United States, like others, is committed to the Rule of Force. The recent World Court incident

was noteworthy only for the clumsiness of the Reagan administration — again, a reflection of its slight departure from the norm.
A government that seeks to increase the power of the state in the
domestic society and to extend its power to use force to achieve its
international goals, as this one does, will naturally tend to be less
refined in its forays into diplomacy.

Again, however, we should be aware that the departure from the
norm is not very great. This particular incident illustrates the point
very well. While ignorant or hypocritical critics of the Reagan
administration (Senator Moynihan for example) denounce it for
departing from the Rule of Law so sacred to the United States — as
illustrated in Moynihan's shenanigans over the illegal U.S. support
for the illegal invasion of Timor, for example — anyone familiar
with U.S. history would understand that the World Court incident
was nothing new. In fact, it is merely a replay of events earlier in the
century, when the United States destroyed the Central American
Court of Justice, which it had established, after the Court ruled
against the United States in the matter of intervention in Nicaragua.
The Court was effectively destroyed by the Wilson administration.
The only crucial difference in the present case is that the United
States is not powerful enough to destroy the World Court.

The UN can do virtually nothing to block the terrorism and
violence of the great powers. The UN can be a useful instrument
when the great powers agree; it can provide mechanisms for them
to achieve their common goals. Apart from that, it could be, and
sometimes is, a useful forum for education; it can help bring to
public awareness and understanding matters that would otherwise
be suppressed. And in areas where neither of the superpowers is
deeply committed to blocking its actions, it can sometimes make an
effective contribution to world peace. But the UN cannot induce the
Soviet Union to relax its grip on Eastern Europe, or induce the
United States to stop tormenting Central America and the
Caribbean. It can easily be blocked by great power sabotage, as
Moynihan's behavior in the case of Timor shows. Similarly, if the
United States determines that there shall be no negotiated
settlement of the Arab–Israeli conflict that grants the indigenous
population any meaningful form of self-determination, there is
nothing the UN can do about it — the efforts of the Secretary
General through 1984 came to naught, because the United States, as
it announced at once, would have no part of a meaningful political
settlement. There are many examples throughout the history of the

United Nations and there is no serious prospect for any change in
this regard.

4

Washington: The Principal Terrorist Government in the World

We have created a more humanitarian, less costly strategy, to be more compatible with the democratic system. We instituted civil affairs [in 1982] which provides development for 70 percent of the population, while we kill 30 percent. Before, the strategy was to kill 100 percent.

General Héctor Gramajo, describing the civil affairs program, employed by the Guatemalan government during the 1980s[1]

The outstanding lesson [of the Vietnam War] is that we should never let another Vietnam-type situation arise again. We were too late in recognizing the extent of the subversive threat. We appreciate now that every young [sic] emerging country must be constantly on the alert, watching for those symptoms which, if allowed to develop unrestrained, may eventually grow into a disastrous situation such as that in South Vietnam. We have learned the need for a strong police force and a strong police intelligence organization to assist in identifying early the symptoms of an incipient subversive situation.

General Maxwell Taylor[2]

---

* This interview was conducted in Frankfurt, April 28, 1986.

Since trade ignores national boundaries and the manufacturer insists on having the world as a market, the flag of his nation must follow him, and the doors of the nations which are closed against him must be battered down. Concessions obtained by financiers must be safeguarded by ministers of state, even if the sovereignty of unwilling nations be outraged in the process. Colonies must be obtained or planted, in order that no useful corner of the world may be overlooked or left unused.

Woodrow Wilson,
President of the United States, 1919[3]

Heinz Dieterich: You just came back from your first trip to Nicaragua. Please describe your experience there.

Noam Chomsky: Well, I was primarily lecturing at the Jesuit University and, of course, traveled a bit and spoke to many people. I was very pleasantly surprised by the openness of Nicaraguan society, the general sense of hopefulness, the range of discussion and also the people's sense that they can somehow withstand the pressures of the American embargo and the terrorist attacks along the borders. I expected to find a much more depressed, closed kind of system. In fact, it is one of the nicest places I have ever visited. I also managed to spend some time with the quite wonderful exile community in Nicaragua — people from all over Central America who fled the various U.S.-sponsored horror chambers. They've settled in Nicaragua, which in fact is one of the few places where a decent person can live with a certain sense of integrity and hope. So, in general, it was quite a stimulating and exciting visit.

HD: What was your most positive experience?

NC: Well, I think the main positive experience was simply the discussions. I had many open discussions with all sorts of people. I gave lectures on a very wide range of topics, anything I felt the least bit competent to speak about (sometimes "least" has to be emphasized). The lectures were broadcast over the radio and were very lively and open. There were many, many people.

I did not manage to travel very much. It was too intense in

Managua. We did a bit. We went to some church-run cooperatives in the countryside and to a few cities. We spent some time at the Ministry of External Affairs with interesting discussions, met some government people, met some of the intellectuals, which was quite interesting.

HD: Did that experience change your attitude towards the revolution in Nicaragua or towards U.S. society and solidarity work?

NC: Well, it changed it in a certain sense. It is always different to see something than to simply read about it. I couldn't say that I learned anything that I basically didn't know, but it added a tone and color that I had not appreciated. I was extremely impressed by the openness of Nicaraguan society. It is difficult to imagine a country at war being that free and open, particularly a country that is being attacked by a superpower.

The United States, which was never attacked during both world wars, imposed restrictive policies of a kind that go beyond anything one encounters in Nicaragua. So, for example, it is inconceivable that the United States would have permitted a newspaper to publish pro-Japanese material during World War II. In fact, the Japanese were all locked up in concentration camps no matter who they were. But *La Prensa,* which is relatively openly pro-Contra, does function.

The place is completely open. You can go anywhere you want and talk about anything you want. They allow representatives of the superpower that's attacking them into the country. Some of the things that happen are just staggering. Right-wing congressmen go to Nicaragua and have press conferences in the airport in which they call for an attack against Nicaragua. It's as if during World War II the United States invited Nazis to come to the United States to have a press conference calling for a bigger attack against the United States. That's simply unimaginable. In fact, during World War I the United States actually locked up a presidential candidate for 10 years, because he made pacifist statements — Eugene Debs, the socialist candidate. The degree of freedom and openness in Nicaragua really surprised me.

HD: Could you expand a bit on the Japanese detentions in the United States during World War II?

NC: Well, in the United States during World War II there were about 100,000 Japanese-Americans, who were not suspected of anything, locked up in concentration camps. Part of that was out of an interest in robbing their land and things like that.

HD: They were U.S. citizens?

NC: Yes, they were American citizens and they were not charged with anything. And recall that the United States was not attacked. American colonies were attacked. Hawaii and the Philippines were colonies and they were bombed. But the United States, of course, was never even under threat of attack. Also, the United States had censorship, they had no-strike requirements and so on. That's what you expect in a country at war. A country at war moves towards totalitarian structures and the United States did. It had a command economy and so on, and it was never under attack.

HD: How do you explain, then, that a first rate power like the United States, which was not under attack, imposed such severe restrictions on civil liberties, while Nicaragua, a third-rate power, which is being attacked by thousands of soldiers, has not done so?

NC: During World War II, the democratic societies made a remarkable shift towards totalitarian structures. In fact, Albert Speer in his memoirs comments on that. He comments on the fact that Germany was never able to institute the kinds of real totalitarian control that the democracies instituted. And, he claims in his memoirs that this set Hitler's war effort back by about a year or something like that. If he is right, that may be the reason why Germany lost the war. But he points out that in the democracies, where the population was committed, they were able to institute real totalitarian controls effectively. Whereas in Germany, where they didn't really trust the population, they had to sort of buy them off.

Nicaragua is a different story. For one thing, Nicaragua was never really a country. Nicaragua was a place robbed by small elite groups and rich people. There was no national unity, there was no sense of Nicaraguan unity, or not very much. The country is really being brought together as a national entity probably for the first time, which raises all sorts of problems. Serious problems of national integration and so on. But to move from an institution for robbing the poor to a country is a major change and it's being done with mistakes, with problems and with successes under horrendous conditions. I don't know exactly how the planning works, but the fact, the very visible fact, is that there is a great sense of openness and hopefulness, alongside other harsher and more unpleasant things.

HD: How would you compare the revolutionary democracy in

Nicaragua with the revolutionary democracy in the United States after it became independent?

NC: Well, the United States was very harsh. First of all, the people who won in the United States were basically terrorists. And, in fact, there are all sorts of aspects of U.S. history which have been pretty much suppressed, even though they took place hundreds of years ago. So, for example, take the question of refugees. The proportion of people who fled from the American colonies after the revolution was actually a higher percentage of the population than the proportion which fled Vietnam. And they were fleeing the richest country in the world. They were fleeing under hard conditions. There were boat people, for example, who fled from Boston in the middle of winter. There were boat people who fled to Nova Scotia, where they died in the snow and they wrote reports about their terrible suffering, and so on. They were fleeing from people they regarded as terrorists. And it was a war that was fought with pea-shooters by contemporary standards. When four people were killed, they called it a "massacre"; four people were killed at the Boston massacre.

During the war, in fact, right in the middle of the war, in 1779, George Washington sent his armies to destroy the most developed native American culture in North America, the Iroquois culture — which in many ways was more advanced than the colonists', except in military terms. It had advanced agriculture and stone dwellings. It was a lively, flourishing civilization. They were, of course, pro-British, because the native population by and large was pro-British. They knew what the colonists had in mind for them and they knew it was genocide. And in the middle of the revolution this culture was wiped out. Now, compare that to all the propaganda about treatment of the Miskitu Indians. It's just a joke.

During the American revolution, the population itself was split. It was a civil war like most revolutionary wars and it was about evenly split. The number of loyalists, that is, pro-British elements, was approximately the same as the number of pro-independence rebels. It was also an international war. The war was basically won by Spain and France. So, in today's terms, you might say that France, assisted by some terrorist units, defeated England in a war. In fact, during the battle of Yorktown, the final battle, the British general handed over his sword to the French commander, not to Washington's troops.

The United States went through a very important development

in the late 18th century. There was a struggle about whether it would be a democracy or not, or what kind of democracy it would be. In the 1780s, during and after the revolution there was a period of true, representative democracy, that is, there were workers and artisans and farmers and so on who took part in the system of representation. That period came to an end at about the turn of the century and the government became a government of the propertied. In fact, the first Chief Justice of the Supreme Court, John Jay, who was President of the Constitutional Congress, put it very succinctly. He said, that the country should be governed by those who own it, and that's literally what happened. Basically the government consisted of propertied white males and it became more and more the property of major investors. At first that meant landowners, later it meant corporations, and so on, and essentially that's what the government became after a struggle in the 18th century. Meanwhile, of course, the country became extremely expansionist, it threw out the native population, or killed them, and that increased through the early 19th century and so we go on. That's true American history, not what's being taught. And, in fact, as everyone knows, a third of Mexico was stolen in the middle of the 19th century.

HD: Given that Nicaragua has not transgressed constitutional and bourgeois-democratic boundaries, how do you explain the United States' insistence on destroying Nicaragua?

NC: Well, the United States doesn't care whether a country has formal democracy. What it cares about is whether it subordinates itself to the U.S.-dominated world system. The primary issue is: Will a country permit itself to be robbed? Will it permit foreign business to invest and exploit at will? If it will do that, it can have any political system it likes. It can be fascist, it can be democratic, it can be communist — whatever you like as long as that criterion is met. But if a country begins to direct its resources to its own population, then it has to be destroyed.

The case of Nicaragua is very similar to the case of, say, Guatemala in the early 1950s. Guatemala was a capitalist democracy. It was mildly reformist, basically modeled on Roosevelt's New Deal. However, it was directing resources to its own domestic population. It was beginning to carry out agrarian reform, it was beginning a successful development and, in general, the social policy was being oriented towards the domestic population. It, too, was turning into a country instead of an area for robbery by its rich elites and foreign businessmen. Therefore, it had to be destroyed, even though it was a capitalist democracy.

In the early 1960s, the Kennedy administration essentially destroyed the Bosch experiment in formal democracy in the Dominican Republic. Bosch was pro-Kennedy. His positions were essentially Kennedy's official positions. Nevertheless, the Kennedy administration undermined them. They backed Trujillo's officers, who overthrew the democratic government in a military coup which Kennedy supported.

And Nicaragua is the same story. The crime of the Sandinistas was to carry out successful development. Right after the revolution they immediately began to divert resources to the poor part of the population. And this, incidentally, is recognized. It's recognized by charitable development agencies, by the international banks and so on. So, for example, the Inter-American Development Bank, in January 1983, wrote a report stating that Nicaragua has made impressive growth advances in socio-economic development and has laid the basis for extensive future growth. That's the crime. Oxfam, the international development organization, has singled out Nicaragua in its own reports, saying that it is unique, that it is exceptional among 76 developing countries in the commitment of its government to social reforms for the benefit of the poor majority and to involving the poor part of the population in the development process. Now, that can't be tolerated. It's a danger. In fact, this Oxfam pamphlet that I was just quoting is called, "Nicaragua: The Threat of a Good Example?" And that's exactly correct.

Think about Honduras, where the population is literally starving to death, as crop lands and forests are being diverted to the production of agricultural exports and the military governs behind a very thin civilian facade. Of course, that causes no problems in the West. Everyone thinks that's wonderful, because the population is starving and they are quiet, and so on and so forth. So, that's fine. But suppose that Honduran peasants can look across the border and see that in a similar country there are health clinics and there is land reform and rural development and so on, they will all immediately begin to ask questions. And that can, in fact, spread. When the administration talks about Nicaragua as a danger, they are quite right. It is a danger.

HD: So, if the key to U.S. policy is property and profit, that would mean that unless Nicaragua returns to a Somoza-kind of robbery they won't live in peace?

NC: Certainly the United States will try to destroy them. However, there are complicated structures in the world. To begin with, there is the U.S. population which is complex and which is imposing constraints. But even in articulate circles there is no understanding of Nicaragua. The elementary facts of the situation cannot be discussed. I am referring to the reports of the World Bank, the International Development Bank, Oxfam and the priests who work there — the facts are not discussed. You are not allowed to talk about them which means that that part of the population which relies on the articulate intelligentsia, the media and other sources do not and cannot have any idea of what is going on.

However, there are other networks; there are church networks, there are independent groups and so on. It's possible to reach substantial elements of the population outside the political system and outside the system of indoctrination. That's what happened during the Vietnam War, in fact. Also, the population in the United States tends to be kind of dissident. It is resistant to authority in many ways, but this is combined with super-patriotism — the mix is complex, but it's there and it's imposing a constraint.

Latin America itself imposes constraints. The United States is concerned that they may lose control of the rest of Latin America if they carry out policies which are too aggressive. Europe is also a concern. Now, Europe has played a rather cowardly role in this. They backed off. They have accepted the orders of the master of the world and are refusing to give any significant help, with a few exceptions. But despite that, American planners are concerned. For example, when American planners read this morning's copy of the *Frankfurter Allgemeine Zeitung* and they see that the Bundestag is taking Gorbachev's proposals for a reduction of forces seriously and says that this is not propaganda, it means something. American planners become concerned because there always has been the possibility that Europe might move towards neutrality, becoming a major rival to U.S. aggression against Nicaragua could increase the likelihood of that occurring; so this also acts as an obstacle, delaying aggressive action.

So there are many complex factors in the world that leave some openings and make it more difficult for the United States. The United States cannot do now what it did in Guatemala in 1954. Then they just overturned the regime and didn't pay any attention to anyone. Now, U.S. power is greater in absolute terms but less in relative terms, as is Soviet power, in fact. The world has just become more complicated.

HD: What are the objectives of the United States in Nicaragua? Is it more convenient for them to destroy the regime and replace it, or to force it to shift from a revolutionary democracy to a revolutionary dictatorship (of the Jacobin type), in order to have a permanent scapegoat like Libya just around the corner?

NC: Well, what the United States would always prefer is something like Honduras. That is, something which has formal democracy. But democracy in the American political lexicon has a very special meaning. It means essentially what John Jay said. Democracy means rule by selected business groups with the population passive and essentially reduced to the role of spectators who are permitted every once in a while to ratify elite decisions. That's democracy. Any move towards popular participation in shaping affairs of state is dangerous. It's not tolerated at home and it's not tolerated abroad. Abroad, you don't tolerate it by sending in the death squads. At home, you have more sophisticated measures to prevent it. But the concern, incidentally, is just as deep at home as it is abroad.

There is very interesting documentation on this. The rise of any form of political consciousness and political participation in the United States causes great fear in liberal circles. In Europe, too, incidentally. There is great fear when there is direct popular involvement. The most striking documentation about this is the report of the Trilateral Commission, which is essentially the liberal elites in Europe, the United States and Japan. The report came out in 1975 and it's called *The Crisis of Democracy*. It describes the fact that in the industrial world in the 1960s, there was a move towards democracy. That is, there was not just the civil rights movement, but the women's movement and the youth movements and the ethnic movements, and so on. That is, normally passive parts of the population began to be engaged in the functioning of the actual system. That's the crisis of democracy and it has to be stopped. The liberal elites agreed that it had to be stopped and they outlined ways of returning the population to the apathy and passivity which is their proper state.

Now, they were talking about the industrial democracies. It's essentially the same concern they had about Central America. In Central America, too, there were the beginnings of popular organizations. There were bible study groups turned into self-help groups. There were peasant unions, teachers unions and so on, and that's the same danger. That's the danger that you might have democracy in a real sense, not elite rule — usually business and landowner rule, with public ratification — but actual participation. Well, as I said, in Central America you send in the death squads. In Germany, France and the United States and elsewhere, you do it in different ways, but you have to repress the threat to democracy.

HD: In the context of analyzing U.S. policy towards Libya you said that the United States is a "gangster state." What did you mean by that?

NC: Well, it's a leading terrorist state. The United States air raid against Libya was one of the major terrorist acts, probably *the* major terrorist act of this year, at least. They killed dozens of people. That's probably five times as many people as can plausibly be attributed to Libyan-sponsored terrorism in the last 10 years. And that's one raid. In fact, if you look at the kinds of charges that are made against Libya and you apply the same standards to the United States, you draw some very interesting conclusions. Libya is accused of involvement in, say, bombing of airplanes, although only a loose connection is evident. But you know, the major terrorist act of 1985 in the Middle East, in terms of the number of people killed, was a car bombing in Beirut where 80 people were killed, which was carried out by people associated with the CIA. Well, the CIA said it wasn't directly involved, so that exculpated them, but there is no proof that Libya was any more involved in the things that are attributed to Libya. These were groups working with the CIA who carried out a bombing and missed somebody and killed 80 people. The biggest terrorist act of 1985 was the bombing of the Air India plane, in which 350 people or so were killed. That was probably carried out by terrorists who were trained in the southern United States. Now, by the standards we apply to Libya, the United States is responsible.

Look at real terrorism, not this small scale terrorism, terrorism like the state terrorism in El Salvador, where a U.S. mercenary army is massacring and slaughtering people at a fantastic rate — maybe 60,000 people in the last six years. Or, take the terrorist army in Guatemala, which the United States has always supported, or the Contras, the leading terrorist force in the world. U.S. terrorist activities against Cuba have also been phenomenal. Since the Kennedy administration, Cuba has been the target of more inter-national terrorism than any other state in the world, probably more than all other states put together, until, say, Nicaragua. What we have here is a major terrorist power. "Gangster state" is an appropriate description.

HD: What's this gangster state going to do in Nicaragua? An intervention with ground troops does not seem very likely at the moment. What's your scenario for the near future? Are they going to do anything?

NC: I think so. First of all, it has to be recognized that there is a real hysterical frenzy on the part of American ruling groups. It's not just concern, it's hysteria. Just take a look at the President's speeches. Of course, he doesn't know what's in them, but the people who write the speeches produce fantastic lies. It's very hard to think of a historical parallel, except maybe for the Nazis or Stalin. So, for example, George Shultz gets on television and says: "Nicaragua is a cancer and we must cut it out." That's hysteria, reminiscent of the way that the Nazis talked in the late 1930s.

What they are trying to do now is to get congressional authorization to escalate the war. The talk about the $100 million is merely a sideshow. They don't care about the money — they can steal it. This is a group of totally lawless people. They'll simply take the money from the CIA budget, illegally. It's just been released, in fact, that the CIA has been directly and illegally funding the Contras for the last several years. The fabricated invasion of Honduras was in part a cover to send $20 million of military aid to the Contras. So the money isn't what counts. What they want is something more symbolic. They want a congressional endorsement of further action. The kind of further action that I would expect is probably moving towards a blockade.

The Contras are probably not a successful terrorist force and I doubt that they can be turned into one. And the United States can't invade directly, because of all sorts of constraints. So, what I suspect they will do is use their technological advantages. High-speed boats, for instance, that can threaten, or maybe attack, shipping. Because of the U.S. embargo, and because of the cowardice of Europe and the backing-off of the Latin Americans, who are frightened, most of the shipping is now probably from the Eastern Bloc: Cuba, Russia, Bulgaria and so on. The United States might try to stop that. They might try to stop it by setting up an international confrontation. That's the arena in which they can hope to win, like the Cuban missile crisis, based on the assumption that the Russians will always back off, which is usually the case. So, I think there's a fair probability of threats to, and maybe direct attacks against,

Cuban or maybe Eastern Bloc shipping using high-speed boats, maybe the Piranhas (the ones which were used to lay the mines and attack the ports).

Now, the Nicaraguans can't respond to that. But Cuba can and Russia can. If they did respond to attacks on their shipping, the United States would probably go into total hysteria and start waving nuclear bombs around, because the United States does not regard it as legitimate for anyone to defend themselves against an American attack. It's quite possible that the Russians will understand that and that the Cubans will understand that, and therefore will not try to defend themselves. If that happens, there will be an effective embargo, an effective blockade imposed. I suspect that planners in Washington are thinking along those lines.

HD: That would leave the Sandinistas no other choice but to spread the war all over Central America. What else could they do?

NC: I don't know what they could do.

HD: Would it mean the beginning of a regionalized war?

NC: That's very hard to predict. For one thing it may lead to nuclear war and there won't be anything else to talk about. If you set up an international confrontation, the world may blow up. American planners have repeatedly been willing to threaten that. For them it's considered a small danger. The idea that the world may blow up is a relatively insignificant consideration as compared with the importance of preventing a small country from using its resources for its own population. That's the way planning works. But it's highly unpredictable — they're playing with stakes that are just too high.

HD: During the Vietnam War, you played an important role in the resistance movement and you were threatened with a jail sentence. I know you don't like to talk about it, but could you, nevertheless, tell us a bit about it?

NC: Well, I was involved in resistance and civil disobedience and so on and in fact I was very likely to face a five year jail sentence. The government was going after people who were organizing resistance and putting them on trial.

But then the Tet Offensive took place and, at that point, government planning changed and business thinking changed. The Tet offensive in January 1968 essentially convinced American elites that the war was too expensive to bother fighting — that it was an investment that should be liquidated. At that point, lots of changes took place. For one thing, a high-level business delegation went to

Washington and essentially ordered Johnson to resign. It was a real power play of a rather striking kind. He resigned.

They then shifted to what they called "Vietnamization" which was a more capital-intensive war, with a reduction of American forces. Part of the reason for that is that the American army was falling apart, much to its credit, I should say. The United States made a tactical error. It's a tactical error to use an army of citizens to fight a colonial war. France sent the French foreign legion — professional killers, ex-Nazis and so on. That's the way you fight a colonial war. You need professional killers, because you are mostly murdering civilians. But a civilian army is not up to the task. They don't have the training and they reflect too much the values of civil society.

When the army began to fall apart, the country was in upheaval and there was a crisis of democracy which greatly concerned the governing elites. So they changed tactics and one of the things that happened was that the prosecutions were stopped. Most of us who were involved in resistance were probably saved from fairly long jail sentences by that decision. And after that, there was normal civil disobedience.

But these are not serious issues. Whatever you might say about the United States, there are some very good things about it. And one of the best things about it is that the state has very limited resources of repression against the relatively privileged parts of the population. And in a rich country like the United States that's a large part of the population. I mean, it's probably the freest country in the world from the point-of-view of the capacity of the state to repress its own citizens by violence. There isn't much in the way of functioning democracy, but there is a lot of freedom. And all of this reflects, essentially, the capitalist character of the country. In a capitalist society, everything is a commodity, including freedom, and you can have as much as you can purchase. And in a rich country you can purchase a lot. If you become an organizer they may kill you, or do something else to you. But if you are part of the relatively privileged elites, and that does include a very substantial part of the population, then you are protected against real government violence. And that's a very important fact.

HD: So that's why you don't like to talk too much about it?

NC: Yes, I don't think it's all that important. And you know, we couldn't really complain if we were sent to jail, because we were asking for it. I mean, if you say, "I am going to resist what they call the law" — what I think is illegal, but they call it "the law" and they run the courts — then of course the government will crack down. It's not a surprise. It's illegitimate force in the sense that the state is illegitimate, but that's a different issue, that's a deeper issue.

HD: Since then, you have kept up the struggle for the poor people, against injustice, repression and so on. What's the driving force behind your engagement? Do you pay a price for it?

NC: Well, first of all, I wouldn't exaggerate the price. It's a very important fact, not to be underestimated, that there are no death squads and there are no psychiatric prisoners and there is no torture and so on. That is not a small fact. One should not forget it. So the price is a different kind of price. It's marginalization, vilification, a little government repression, an awful lot of time and so on. But those are not real costs. We live in the major terrorist state in the world. We are oppressing, torturing, murdering, causing people to starve. We are doing horrendous things. At the very least, there's a moral responsibility to try to protect victims from the violence of your own state. That's what it comes down to.

5

Irangate:
Trading with the Enemy

... from Oxfam's experience of working in seventy-six developing countries, Nicaragua was to prove exceptional in the strength of that Government's commitment... to improving the condition of the people and encouraging their active participation in the development process...

Diana Melrose, *Nicaragua: The Threat of a Good Example?*
1985[1]

Heinz Dieterich: I'd like to ask you some questions about "Irangate," because everybody's confused about it. The first thing is why are things that Reagan has been doing for years suddenly being called a scandal? Lying, abusing power and things like that. Why is this suddenly a problem?

Noam Chomsky: I think there are several reasons for that. One reason is that it was impossible to keep it undercover. First, the Hasenfus plane was shot down and then the Iranians announced — first in Beirut and then in Iran — that McFarlane[2] had been there.

---

* This interview was conducted in March 1987.

Both of those stories were too big. It was simply impossible to keep it quiet. So it hit the newspapers.

Israel had been providing arms to Iran for years with U.S. support — since 1980, in fact, and everybody knew about it. But it was sort of suppressed as an issue. I wrote a lot about it in *Fateful Triangle*, but nobody paid attention of course. But now with McFarlane showing up in Teheran and with a Contra plane being shot down with an American in it. That's just impossible to keep quiet. So the thing just came out and once it comes out, then you can do damage control, but you can't keep everything quiet.

The second issue is that once it became public, a fact which had long been suppressed also became public, namely that the executive branch was defying congressional legislation. Congress represents a system of power and they're going to defend themselves. They don't care about violating ICJ proceedings or anything like that. As long as the issue of secret supply to the Contras could be kept quiet, they didn't really care. But once it becomes a public matter that the executive branch is snubbing its nose at Congress, they can't tolerate that, and they have to somehow defend their rights because they do represent substantial power, diverse but substantial. That's essentially what the Tower Commission Report's about.[3] It's very narrowly focused on procedural issues. It really had to do with congressional authority, the constitutional system and so on. After all, business wants to keep that system alive.

The third point, which is probably the most important one, had to do with the ideological system. All of these guys had built up international terrorism as the central thing; that's the way you control the population — by frightening them with international terrorism. It was the centerpiece of the ideological system in the 1980s — we need missiles and we need to lower the standard of living and we need all of this kind of stuff to defend ourselves against international terrorism. Part of that is the claim that we're never going to deal with terrorists. But then, all of a sudden it turns out that the Reagan administration *is* dealing with a terrorist state. That blows the whole ideological system out of the water. That's intolerable. In fact, if you look carefully, you'll notice that that's the thing they're all upset about. How could we be doing that? We're supposed to be defending everyone against terrorists. The contradictions are just too great. You start getting people to understand that the whole business is a fraud and you're in trouble. So it has to be some kind of mistake or something. But anyway, you can't suppress it, it's just too vivid a contradiction and I think that's essentially it.

Of course, all the commentary in the media and everywhere else avoids the main issues. First of all, no one is raising any questions about the propriety of funding the Contras, the propriety of violating the World Court decision, any of this stuff — that's all off the agenda. Furthermore, the background to the Iran stuff is also off the agenda. Nobody has confronted the first question that springs to mind if you want to understand the post-1985 Iran supplies: what was happening before 1985? The answer is that before 1985 the United States was supplying arms to Iran via Israel. What's more, they were very open about why they were doing it. They were doing it to try to carry off a military coup. In fact it's just a replay of Chile and Allende, Indonesia and Sukarno, Brazil and Goulart in 1964 and thousands of other examples.

When you have hostile relations with a country, with a state, what you try to do is establish connections to the military in the hope that they'll overthrow it. And it works. Pinochet and Suharto worked. They were hoping that this one would work. The way you establish contacts with the military is by sending arms and training, that kind of stuff. In fact if you look carefully at the Tower Commission Report, sort of hidden inside it you find that they were very concerned that the arms they were sending got to the professional military not the Pasdaran [revolutionary guards]. Because they know that those guys are not their types. They want to strengthen the role of the professional military.

In February 1979, right after the Shah left Iran, the U.S. head of Nato command, General Huyser, went to Iran to try to set off a military coup. Carter sent him to find some generals who would get the thing under control before Khomeini came in. But they couldn't do it, they were too demoralized. It was impossible, the place would have blown up. So he backed off. The right wingers here, like Brzezinski and Kirkpatrick and Marty Peretz and those guys, have been screaming for years that we lost our chance because we didn't carry off a military coup at that time.

Right after that, Israel and the United States responded in the obvious way: they began establishing relations with the military in the hope of finding generals or colonels or anybody who could do it for them. What apparently happened is that their contacts in the military were caught and executed in 1984 and then they had to find another track — and it's this one. But none of this stuff is ever going to be discussed. You can bet your life on that.

HD: Sometimes the newspapers ask whether there is a problem with the U.S. political system. Is there something structurally wrong? What does this affair tell us about the U.S. political system?

NC: It tells us essentially nothing that we didn't know. The executive branch is committed to international terrorism. They call it "counterinsurgency," or "low-intensity war," or one thing or another. Congress essentially agrees, but it does to some extent reflect a wider range of opinion and it's concerned about the possibility of failure. The whole debate about Nicaragua now is very narrow. It's: "Will the Contras succeed?" For example, if the Contras succeeded in capturing a city — they're not going to, but suppose they did — congressional opposition would collapse immediately. And the Contras understand that. Their spokesman here keeps saying, "Look, you just keep supplying us and we'll win a military success." That's their line, and they say that because they understand the United States very well. The only thing that matters is, "Is it going to work?"

As far as the political system is concerned it doesn't tell you a damn thing. It tells you that if congressional authority is violated openly and publicly, they will move to try to reassert it. That's the way the political system works — same in Watergate. What was the big fuss in Watergate? Well, they broke into the Democratic Party headquarters. The Democrats are a system of organized power, they're going to defend themselves. You can destroy the Socialist Workers Party through the FBI if you want, but not the Democrats.

HD: An issue which is hotly debated in Mexico and all over Latin America is the implication of Irangate for U.S. policy towards Nicaragua.

NC: Well, my own feeling is that it's probably inhibited them for a while at least, because there's just too much embarrassment. On the other hand, in the longer term I don't think there's any effect. Their assumption is that if they can't stop the Sandinistas through the Contras, they'll ultimately have to do something else. Whatever it'll be, maybe invasion.

HD: You consider that a serious possibility?

NC: Not really. I think a naval blockade is much more likely.

HD: But you're quite serious that this could happen?

NC: Oh yeah. Carlucci, the Defense official, has been talking about it.

HD: Is it possible to say anything about the likely timing of such an event, or is that impossible?

NC: A lot depends on things that I can't judge. Like what the military successes or failures of the Contras will be. I don't know how to judge that. But if they don't get anywhere and they look like they're just collapsing militarily, the Congress and others here will be upset because it's going to be costly to us, and then they're going to have to turn to another course, and the obvious course is a blockade.

HD: What does Irangate mean for Reagan's presidency?

NC: Again it's hard to say. It depends on how well the public relations system works. Take Watergate, for example. If it hadn't been for the exposure of the 18 minutes of erased tape, Nixon would have weathered it. It was sort of out of order. When that came out, it was just too much and then they couldn't save him, so they sacrificed him and got somebody else. Maybe something like that will happen with Reagan — who knows. They may find some scandal that they just can't live with, in which case they'll sacrifice Reagan who amounts to nothing anyway; he's just a public relations creation. Short of that, I suppose, they'll try to go after lower guys. North[1] will be in jail for a couple of years or something and then be reconstructed.

But, undoubtedly the presidency is weakened, that is, other interests are now somewhat willing to assert themselves and that may weaken the Reaganites' power in a limited way in the next couple of years. Since they're all basically within the same framework of assumptions, I don't think it matters all that much.

HD: Have the chances of the Republican party being reelected in two years dimmed, or are they the same?

NC: At the moment, I suppose they have dimmed a little bit. Again, I think it's a matter of tenth order significance, since they are basically all following the same policies.

6

Cuba:
"Ripe for the Picking"
by the United States

[Guatemala] has become an increasing threat to the stability of Honduras and El Salvador. Its agrarian reform is a powerful propaganda weapon; its broad social program of aiding the workers and peasants in a victorious struggle against the upper classes and large foreign enterprises has a strong appeal to the populations of Central American neighbors where similar conditions prevail.

U.S. State Department official, 1954[1]

[Cuba] is being watched closely by other nations in the hemisphere and any appearance of success there would have an extensive impact on the statist trend elsewhere in the area.

CIA report, 1964[2]

...there is a consensus among scholars of a wide variety of ideological positions that, on the level of life expectancy, education and health, Cuban achievement is considerably greater than one would expect from its level of per capita income. A recent study of 113 Third World countries in terms of these basic indicators of popular welfare ranked Cuba first, ahead even of Taiwan... What has changed remarkably is not so much the gross indicators as those that reflect the changed conditions of the poor. In 1958,

---

* This interview was conducted in October 1991.

for example, the one rural hospital in the entire country represented about 2 percent of the hospital facilities in Cuba; by 1982 there were 117 hospitals, or about 35 percent of all hospitals in Cuba.

Tom Farer, former U.S. State Department
assistant for inter-American affairs[3]

Heinz Dieterich: How significant is the Soviet Union's withdrawal of its troops from Cuba?
Noam Chomsky: The withdrawal of troops, as such, is of no major significance because their presence was basically symbolic. What is very important is the withdrawal of economic subsidies.
HD: What will be the consequences?
NC: In 1959–60, the Eisenhower administration made an explicit decision to overthrow the Cuban government. There are planning documents from March 1960 and, later, from the Kennedy administration, that document this decision. The United States employed methods that ranged from a widespread campaign of terrorism to direct invasion. When the invasion failed, the terrorism campaign was intensified. This included economic strangulation, a cultural quarantine and the intimidation of anyone who attempted to break Cuba's isolation. Obviously, no small country can resist such attacks.

The situation is even more difficult in the case of Cuba because of its historic relationship with the United States. In fact, it had been colonized by, and was entirely dependent on, the United States. But even a truly independent country would have been incapable of enduring such an attack. Cuba only survived because of its relationship with Eastern Europe. The relationship was inefficient and very costly, but at least it allowed Cuba to survive. Ever since the Soviet Union began to collapse and disappear from the world stage, one of the United States' main objectives has been to achieve an end to support for Cuba by the Soviet Union and its former allies

— leaving Cuba to fall into U.S. hands. During the 1980s, relations with Cuba were presented as the real test of Gorbachev's new thinking. That is, the answer to the question of whether Gorbachev was really serious, or whether the Cold War would continue, was supposedly to be found in his aid to Cuba.

Obviously, it is considered totally illegitimate to help someone that the United States wants to destroy. The reasoning is simple: everything that the United States does is right, by definition. Therefore, anyone who interferes with what the United States does is, by definition, wrong. This is the primary assumption that everyone accepts. And so the proof of Gorbachev's new thinking, and its seriousness, consisted in whether or not he would allow the destruction of Cuba.

It's surprising how old themes persist. I've always thought that the East–West conflict was misinterpreted, given that the conflict was, at its root, a North–South one. But it's amazing how themes born during the first days of the U.S. republic continue totally unchanged. Thomas Jefferson and John Quincy Adams, both "founding fathers," spoke of the need to incorporate Cuba into the nascent U.S. empire. Jefferson wanted simply to annex it. But in those days they couldn't do it because an obstacle existed. And the obstacle at that time was England. The English fleet made it impossible for the United States to simply conquer and annex Cuba.

The theory held by everyone at the time was that Cuba, following what John Quincy Adams called "the laws of political gravitation," would fall into our hands like a "ripe fruit." Let's wait for the fruit to ripen and fall into our hands. That was precisely why the United States was always against Cuba liberating itself from Spain. The United States exercised enormous pressure on Mexico, Colombia and others to prevent Cuba's liberation. Bolívar[4] was all too aware of this and was very saddened by it. But from the U.S. point-of-view, its position made sense. If Cuba achieved its independence, it would not fall into its hands like ripe fruit. They were also very worried about democratic tendencies and liberation movements in Cuba, which aimed to liberate slaves and struggle for equality for Afro-Cubans, all of which was intolerable for the empire. Therefore, for various reasons, the United States was opposed, from the early 1800s, to the liberation of Cuba. It maintained this position until, at the end of the century, it in fact conquered Cuba and made it a colony, under the pretext of liberating it from Spain. And it effectively continued as a U.S. colony until the government of Fidel Castro came to power in 1959.

Of course, hostilities by the United States began immediately. In late 1959, the CIA was already involved in subversive activities. In March 1960, the Eisenhower administration had produced the secret documents mentioned above. They said their objective was to replace the Castro regime with one "more devoted to the true interests of the Cuban people and more acceptable to the U.S." And it continued: this must be done "in such a manner as to avoid any appearance of U.S. intervention." This was already the *leitmotif* of our policy in March 1960. Kennedy continued this policy and it has been perpetuated to this day, because we have to make sure that the ripe fruit falls into our hands.

We can overlook the bit about "the true interests of the Cuban people" — it doesn't deserve a comment. But as far as the second part — "a government more acceptable to the U.S." and the avoidance of an "appearance of U.S. intervention" — there is a reason: Latin American countries must be able to pretend that they don't know what is going on. It is difficult for the rulers of Latin American countries to openly approve violent intervention by the United States. From that, a consensus is born. We pretend that no U.S. intervention exists and the Latin American governments pretend to believe it. That is how hemispheric affairs are carried out. With the policy of the embargo, the cultural quarantine, possibly sabotage, and with external support for Cuba declining, the United States assumes that Latin American regimes will be too intimidated by the boss of the hemisphere to break with this policy. Europe and Japan could do it but, again, the issue is not important enough for them to warrant confronting the United States.

HD: Is it possible that the United States will take advantage of these circumstances by launching a military operation, as in Iraq?

NC: I think this will depend to a large extent on the U.S. domestic political situation and the situation within Cuba. We don't have access to the actual secret plans of the elite but they can be surmised. Obviously, they suppose that with the policy of strangulation the situation in Cuba will severely worsen. And, as the situation deteriorates, there will naturally be protests which, in turn, will bring about repression. The activities of the repressive apparatus will grow ever more rigorous, due to the growing effects of the policy of strangulation, and then we will have the natural cycle of more repression, more dissidence and, perhaps, violence. Cuban exiles will land, they will create more problems and at some stage the United States could invade.

The United States will not invade Cuba while it considers that there will be armed resistance. It will not attack someone who can defend themselves. That is obvious. The idea is to "liberate" the country at no cost to U.S. interests, that is, to wait until the internal situation is so bad that U.S. troops can invade without much opposition — or, possibly, with the approval of the population, unable to stand the situation any longer.

HD: Like in Panama?

NC: Yes, Panama is a good example. You keep torturing people until they finally accept you, like a liberation. And one has to understand this, because the situation is so horrible that the only way to survive is under the domination of the colossus of the North. There will be many factors which will determine whether the United States invades Cuba or not — U.S. domestic issues, for example. The Bush administration may decide that it needs a foreign policy triumph before the next election. One of the principal enemies of the government is the U.S. population. It must be controlled. They must not be allowed to see the social catastrophes that surround them. And the classic way to do this is to produce chauvinist hysteria by means of cheap victories. It is important that they be cheap.

There was an awesome demonstration of this in Iraq. Military operations were designed so that no battles took place. At the headquarters of the First Mechanized Division in Fort Riley, Kansas, a reporter for *Newsday* newspaper recently discovered the following. When U.S. troops entered Kuwait they were led by a battalion of engineers driving bulldozers. These were used to bury possibly thousands of Iraqi soldiers alive in their trenches. They simply drove the bulldozers over the trenches and buried the soldiers alive. This is a horrible war crime, but nobody cares. Nonetheless, it does reveal something about U.S. military planning. If you attack someone who can defend themselves, you don't send bulldozers into battle. This makes it clear that the United States had prepared everything in such a way that there was never going to be a war. And, effectively, there never was a war, there never was a battle, only slaughter and atrocities.

Well, this is the way to conduct a war and become heroes and create chauvinist hysteria. Hitler understood this and the whole world understands it. Cheap victories are the trick.

7

The United States and the Future of Cuba

[Cuba is] an object of transcendent importance to the commercial and political interests of our union.

John Quincy Adams, U.S. Secretary of State [1]

The democratic process doesn't always produce perfect results.

Robert Torricelli, Chairman of House Foreign Affairs subcommittee on Western Hemisphere affairs, commenting on U.S. removal of democratically-elected President Aristide from Haiti[2]

There is a tacit collaboration between the Haitian military and the State Department. The Americans will have the last word. And the Americans don't want Aristide's return.

Haitian Consul in New York[3]

Those 2,000 hard-core guys [maintained by the United States in the operations against Nicaragua] could keep some pressure on the Nicaraguan government, force them to use their economic resources for the military, and prevent them from solving their economic problems and that's a plus... Anything that puts pressure on the Sandinista regime, calls attention to the lack of democracy, and prevents the Sandinistas from solving their economic problems is a plus.

U.S. Defense Department official, 1988[4]

---

* This interview was conducted in January 1992.

Heinz Dieterich: Did the execution of the terrorist Betancourt weaken or strengthen Cuba's position?
Noam Chomsky: I think it weakened it. More to the point, it is a reflection of Cuba's weakness. The United States is increasing pressure and getting ready to come in for the kill. By the way, this clearly shows, if any confirmation was needed, the lie in the claim that the United States was against Cuba because of the Cold War.

The official doctrine regarding antagonism towards Cuba over the last 30 years has been that it was a tentacle of the "Evil Empire" and that we have to defend ourselves from the Russians. Well, now they can't even claim that.

And the effect of this abandonment of all pretensions is that the United States has intensified its pressure against Cuba, which demonstrates to any rational person that the Cold War never had anything to do with this problem. What did have something to do with this antagonism was Cuba's independence, which the United States will, of course, never tolerate. This goes back to the 1820s. The United States opposed Cuba's independence in Simón Bolívar's day and continues to oppose it today, for the same reasons.

But the more Washington sees the possibility of crushing Cuba and sending it back to the old days — when it could be exploited by U.S. corporations, the Mafia, and so on — the more it closes off economic space and increases terrorist activities. At least, it seems to me that this is the meaning of the last incident with the terrorists.

By becoming more repressive, Cuba is reacting in exactly the way the United States wants it to. In some ways that reaction is understandable, but nevertheless it's still a mistake.
HD: If the reaction was a mistake, what should they have done?
NC: I think they could have jailed those people. That would have been appropriate, because they were detained for a terrorist act. And Cuba could have taken advantage of this opportunity to expose U.S. terrorism. But instead of doing this, they executed one of them, giving the United States the chance to swap roles and denounce Cuba for its inhumane behavior.
HD: In 1961, discussions took place in Cuba about what to do with more than 1000 terrorist mercenaries captured in the Bay of Pigs. Obviously they couldn't execute the lot of them and if they were kept prisoner for many years, the United States would undertake an irresistible propaganda campaign to free them.

So, it was decided to force the country which sent them to pay ransom. In Betancourt's case, which is very different, Cuba opted for execution. Was that a mistake?

NC: Yes, it was an error now and it would have been an error then. To begin with, it's a mistake to execute people because it gives the United States a powerful propaganda weapon. And, in any case, it's not right to do it. Aside from any other consideration, you shouldn't kill people. In fact, I sent a telegram to Cuba just like I do for Amnesty International's campaigns against capital punishment and death sentences. I do it for any country, including the United States. The United States uses the death penalty constantly and almost always against Afro-Americans. Thus, the United States has no basis upon which to condemn anybody else who also does it. However, the application of the death penalty is inherently bad and also politically and tactically wrong. It is, in fact, exactly what the Bush government wants — it wants Cuba to be more repressive. The aim of the economic strangulation, of the cultural quarantine and of the recurring terrorism is, to a large extent, to foster larger scale repression within Cuba. Like in Nicaragua. You want the country to be very repressive because it gives you an excuse to continue doing that which made it repressive. This is a classic tactic.

HD: How could the Cuban government fall into what you consider to be a trap?

NC: I think that they feel they're trapped and to a certain extent they are. To be honest, there's not much they can do. If they follow the road of democratization, if they establish closer relations with Europe and Latin America, and so on, then there might be a small chance that Cuba would escape U.S. pressure. But I think this is a very slight possibility, because the United States is so powerful that nobody will interfere with its plans.

HD: The State Department says that it will not allow any more terrorist excursions from Miami. Can this be taken seriously?

NC: You can take it as seriously as you took it 30 years ago. If they want to stop terrorist activities in Miami, they can do it. But they've never been interested in stopping them and they're not interested now. It wouldn't surprise me in the least if they were fostering and organizing the terrorist activities. That is very likely. We will find out in 30 years.

HD: What is the significance of the contrast between the U.S. policy of aggression against Cuba and its soft policy in relation to Haiti?

NC: In reality there is no contrast; it's actually the same policy. In Haiti's case the United States hasn't taken even the most basic measures, such as freezing the fortunes of the coup leaders that are kept in U.S. banks. That doesn't even require an embargo; all they have to do is freeze their funds. It would be a measure that would hit them where it truly hurts them. But the United States won't do it and precisely for the same reasons that it wants to crush Cuba. The Haitian elites are the kind of people that we want in power. And we want them in power in Cuba as well. So, the policies towards Cuba and Haiti are entirely consistent.

HD: Is this why they don't support Aristide?

NC: The earliest documents relating to the overthrow of Castro, dating back to March 1960, are very revealing in this respect. During the Eisenhower administration, the National Security Council approved a resolution mandating the overthrow of the Cuban regime and stipulating that it must be done in a way that does not implicate the United States. That is most important, because the United States has to conserve its credibility among Latin American states. Obviously, U.S. allies in the region are aware, but it's very important for them to be able to pretend they don't know what it's doing. Because if they know, then they have to answer to their own population. That is why the United States carries out subversion and terrorism under a guise — this way its allies can pretend that they don't know anything. I imagine that this is the reason for the State Department statement you mentioned. It basically means: yes, we'll continue to do as we have done until now, but in such a way that the region's rulers can pretend that they're not aware.

HD: Can you see the United States taking military action?

NC: That depends in part on the domestic political situation. The Bush government is trying to build some kind of economic recovery before the elections, some kind of temporary recovery so that Bush can say that the situation is improving. After 10 years of economic mismanagement by Reagan and Bush, the economy is in a bad state. No one knows if they can make it recover or not. But if they can't do it, they'll need to come up with something extravagant in foreign policy. Foreign policy adventures have the effect of frightening and mobilizing the population. During war the population lines up behind the leader and the flag and this happens regularly, every two or three years. It's simply a concomitant of economic policies directed against the well-being of the majority of the population. The two things go together like Siamese twins.

So, if they don't succeed in fixing up the economy, then they will try to come up with some foreign policy success and the obvious candidate would be Cuba. You could start writing the editorials already: "We've liberated Cuba," "Utopia is here," "The whole hemisphere is democratic," and so on. Domestic factors could accelerate the process, but I think the rational plan entails waiting for Cuba to collapse. If you maintain the embargo, impede contacts, make sure nobody does anything of importance to break the isolation, maintain the cultural quarantine, then the result within Cuba will be suffering — and suffering equals dissidence, protests and rebellion. This will lead to more repression, the people on the streets will be shot at, leading to more resistance and you reach a point at which civil society self-destructs. Then you can send the marines and the people will applaud because everything is falling down. This is the "correct" way of going about it.

HD: Here there are big solidarity movements who collect money to send oil to Cuba. Is their work going in the right direction?

NC: It's the right direction. Given that governments will not do what needs to be done, the task of civil society is to counter U.S. policy. It's similar to what happened in Nicaragua. You will not succeed in getting governments to resist the U.S. attacks, but you can motivate the people to do it. And you can achieve far from trivial results. These things have to be done in Europe, where they would be much more relevant because it's much wealthier. It's crucially important to do such things in the United States, but sadly they don't happen.

HD: And was the recent congress in solidarity with Cuba in New York a weak or strong start?

NC: As was to be expected, the congress was treated as a scandal by the press and the anti-Cuban protesters were the heroes. It was very similar to the Vietnam protests in the 1960s. The protesters were the disruptive ones and the counter-demonstrators were the heroes who were defending freedom.

We have a Cuban exile community dying to taking over Cuba. There is a lot of strong interest from businessmen, including criminal interests. Remember that Cuba was one of the main centers of Mafia activity [before the revolution]. Remember also that we have had 30 years of anti-Cuba propaganda and that Cuba has been one of the principal themes of U.S. foreign policy since 1820. Well, nothing has changed.

8

The Future
of the Third World

Central America today is experiencing globalization, a more devastating pillage than what its people underwent 500 years ago with the conquest and colonization... [The dominant force is not the market but rather] a strong transnational state that dictates economic policy and plans resource allocation. The IMF, World Bank, Interamerican Development Bank, U.S. Agency for International Development, European Community, UN Development Program and their ilk are all state or interstate institutions of a transnational character that have much greater economic influence over our countries than the market.

Report at Jesuit Conference in San Salvador, January 1994[1]

America is not doing very well, but its corporations are doing just fine.

New York Times **business article:**
"Paradox of '92: Weak Economy, Strong Profits"[2]

---

* This interview was conducted in December 1993.

Heinz Dieterich: Is it possible for contemporary capitalism to provide the majority of humanity with an acceptable standard of living?

Noam Chomsky: Well, I don't think that's its purpose. Current plans and objectives envisage that a very substantial part of the world's population, which could easily turn out to be the great majority, will be marginalized. The Third World model, named after the place where this paradigm is already functioning, is extending itself gradually to the wealthy societies. That is an almost inevitable consequence of the internationalization of production.

In fact, the business press is quite frank about this. Look, for example, at what they write about the end of the Cold War. The business press understands it well — it doesn't play ideological games. It knows that it essentially means the return of Eastern Europe to the Third World and emphasizes that this offers new and great opportunities for international corporations. For example, the London *Financial Times,* the best international business newspaper and quite liberal in nature, recently carried an article with the headline "Green Shoots in Communism's Ruins." It describes how the unemployment caused by the market reforms offer Western businesses labor that is cheap, educated and easily exploitable, which will in turn undermine the demands of the supposedly "pampered" Western workers, who insist on vacations, wages and other benefits. This is the standard line throughout the business press. Workers are told: "If you demand higher wages, then we will go to Taiwan or Mexico." All this is part of the internationalization of production, it's an automatic consequence of it.

Possibly they won't transfer jobs overseas — I don't believe what some people say about the [North American] Free Trade Agreement [NAFTA]. I don't think that it will have any major effect on jobs, but it does give these businesses a weapon and it's a weapon against the U.S. worker. At the core, the message to workers is: "We don't need you any more. We needed you during the times of the national economy." During the 1920s, for example, Henry Ford had to pay his workers decent wages otherwise they couldn't buy his cars. But in a more international economy, that becomes less of a necessity. Not only do you no longer need your "pampered" Western worker as a labor force, it also becomes less clear whether you need it as a market for consumption. Production can take place in countries with high levels of repression and low salaries and it can be directed to the rich of the world. The sector that is a part of the modern world is much bigger in New York, Paris or London than it is in Mexico City or Sao Paulo. But together, the rich at an international level constitute a substantial market and maybe the rest of the population won't be needed.

HD: If contemporary capitalism is not a viable option for the majority of humanity, can it be reformed in such a way that it does become one?

NC: Well, anything can be reformed. And, of course, reforms do change things. There probably will be something that replaces capitalism. But, all of this really has nothing to do with capitalism. We are very far from anything that could be given that name. Analyze, for example, the notion of the market. We have nothing remotely resembling one. If you research international trade, probably 40 percent of it has nothing to do with trade. It is simply an exchange within the same company — for example, Ford sending something from one subsidiary to another. This has nothing to do with trade. It's as if someone who has a small vegetable store moved a can of beans from one shelf to another. It's just that this takes place across international borders, but it doesn't have anything to do with trade; it's an organized act by a centralized management. The Free Trade Agreement is a good example. All you have to do is look at who is in favor of it and obviously it's the big corporations. But they're in favor of it because it means protectionism. Listen to what they are saying on national radio, for example, where they frankly explain why NAFTA is so fantastic. The Treaty has 200 pages of rules of origin provisions that will strengthen our position against industries based in Asia and Europe. If those industries undertake reprisals, which they will do sooner or later, it will be against our protectionism. In fact, NAFTA is a reprisal against the protectionism of the European Community. And if they do take reprisals, it won't bother us too much because we're already inside their systems. Workers, on the other hand, will be considerably affected.

There are many economic models about the effects of the Free Trade Agreement and the international free market, but among the many reasons why they make virtually no sense is the fact that they don't take any of these considerations into account. Nevertheless, protectionist proposals such as those in NAFTA are absolutely reasonable for centrally managed institutions like the ones that have to a large extent taken over from what was the capitalist market. The world market system has very little in common with a capitalist system. Some people have called it "corporate mercantilism," which is probably more accurate. We all know that a corporation doesn't operate internally according to market principles. Within General Motors, for example, there isn't a market system. The organization is centralized, has strategic planning, and so on and so forth. Well, this type of organization represents a good part of the international economy, probably half of it.

Such issues have been part of traditional economic theory but, of course, they are beyond the considerations of World Bank economists. In classical theory, there was a free market model and within it existed businesses like small stores, and so on. Internally, these businesses did not operate according to the free market, but they constituted only very small points within the system, like islands in the sea of the free market. But now these islands have become as big as the sea, and the sea never did operate as a free market anyway.

If you read David Ricardo and Adam Smith on the principles of the free market, they saw the unrestricted flow of labor as something crucial. Without the free movement of the labor force, there is no free market. Ricardo also presupposed the immobility of capital. His whole model of comparative advantages is based on the immobility of capital and the mobility of labor. Therefore, when we talk about current free market models, we are not talking about models that don't quite fit reality — we're talking about models that have nothing to do with reality at all.

This does not mean that these models are not applied. They're imposed on the poor, they're imposed on the Third World. Their economies are subjected to structural adjustments that are, in fact, something like a modified free market system and those economies have, of course, collapsed.

There is not a single example in history of a developed society which has followed free market rules. The historical record is absolutely consistent. From England and the United States, to Japan and South Korea, all developed societies, without exception, have radically violated these principles. And those who were forced to follow them, like Ireland or India under the British, or South Africa or Sub-Saharan Africa... well, all you need to do is take a look at them to see the state they're in. Strategic planners have always known that this is the truth. And economists have interests that induce them to be part of this. They don't get paid if they don't participate. The only country from the South that is a part of the G-7 group is Japan. Why? Because it was never colonized. And some of its colonies are in tow because they were able to defend themselves from the international market system. They never accepted its rules. They are centrally planned, they are societies with very powerful states that control capital and the labor force. That's why they were able to impose development.

It's amazing how all this works. Recently, there was a long front page article in the *New York Times* entitled, "An Introduction to Free Trade." It was basically teaching the poor, uneducated masses why free trade is so important. The article quoted in capital letters a letter from 300 economists that said: we're all in favor of this because it is all proven and, naturally, it's all mathematical so it's difficult to expect that you will understand it. And they quote Paul Samuelson about how free international trade leads to maximum efficiency in the use of resources. And that, in fact, they have verified it.

But no one bothers to point out the consequences. Suppose that their assertion is true and that it was also the case 150 years ago, because it's a universal truth. Then, when the United States imposed, around 1830, very high tariffs to exclude English textile imports, thereby allowing the development of its textile industry near Boston, this interfered with the efficient use of economic resources. But it created the basis for a manufacturing system in the United States. In fact, economic historians have estimated that without those high protection tariffs, around 50 percent of manufacturing in the New England states would have fallen into bankruptcy instantly.

Let's look at the steel industry at the end of the 19th century. Why do we have a steel industry? Because British steel was excluded. And this allowed Andrew Carnegie to found and develop a corporation worth billions of dollars. And if we move on to the 20th century, why do we have computers and electronics? Because the government created them. It poured taxpayers' money into them, because the inefficiency of the market didn't allow their development. Therefore, if the United States had followed the teachings on the free market, which the economists are so kind to give to us, today it would be exporting furs. And, without a free market policy, India would possibly have carried out the industrial revolution. But no one bothers to point this out.

Returning to the question of whether capitalism can be modified, the first answer is that we don't even have capitalism. But the question that really should be asked is: "What can we do in a world in which the centralization of authority over the economic and political system is reaching higher and higher levels and is increasingly distant from any degree of public influence and control?" The internationalization of production has two clear consequences. One is that the Third World model returns home and the other is that it generates new governing structures. National governments have become integrated, in some ways, around the national economies and the international government is becoming integrated around an international economy. The IMF [International Monetary Fund], the World Bank, the G-7 group,[3] GATT [General Agreement on Tariffs and Trade],[4] the European Community executive, etc., are basically the fundamentals of an international government. And there are no controls over this. One has to adhere to it, because that's where the power is. And the beauty of this system is that the public is completely excluded. There is no threat of democracy. The public doesn't even know what is going on. Who, for example, is aware of what goes on inside GATT? Everything goes on in total secret, with the population completely excluded.

There are some other aspects of the internationalization of the economy that I have not mentioned. For example, during the past 20 years there has been a big increase in the amount of unregulated international capital basically used for speculation and financial transactions, not for trade and production. The numbers in this respect are amazing. It was estimated that for the year 1970, some 90 percent of international capital was used for trade and production and 10 percent for speculation. Today, these numbers have probably been inverted. And the result of this is that governments are virtually forced to carry out anti-inflationary policies, because this is what international speculators prefer. They want money to be stable. European countries can't defend their currencies. Everybody knows that. But even in a country as wealthy as the United States something similar takes place. When Clinton tried to introduce a modestly stimulating budget, it was knocked-back immediately. The owners of bonds, securities, etc., want low inflation. And this is reflected in the reduction of growth rates. These are very dire circumstances for any kind of social-democratic government that comes to power.

HD: What is the most important task for humanity? Democratizing this system, or changing it radically?

NC: Both things, because democratization *would* mean a radical change of current conditions. The rebuilding of democratic institutions really implies radical changes.

HD: Would it be necessary to put forward such a program on a worldwide basis? Who could develop this program? Trade union leaders, intellectuals, nongovernment organizations?

NC: Generally speaking, the big intellectuals wouldn't participate. And there are very good structural reasons for this. You will never be a respected intellectual if you don't serve the interests of those in power. You will be left out, marginalized. But, some intellectuals should be a part of this. In fact, it's their job to build an alternative to the system, even if only to protect their own lives, communities, values, future generations, and so on, because we really are moving toward a very ugly international system. An international Third World is not a pretty prospect.

HD: What is your opinion of post-modernism?

NC: I think that it is part of the way in which the intellectual community carries out its work of marginalizing and confusing people. I don't mean to say that it doesn't make any sense at all, but I do think that something like 90 percent of it is a total delusion. And that is very useful. It maintains the intellectuals' positions and so on.

HD: Is it basically the production of ideology?

NC: It is really difficult for me to comment, because most of it doesn't even make sense. I don't think I'm dumber than the average person, because I can understand other difficult things. But when I look at this stuff my eyes glaze over. What are they talking about? When I do understand what they are talking about, which is rare, I just find truisms. For example, the idea that there are no firm foundations of knowledge is something that has been obvious for 300 years.

Other stuff is simply nonsense, for example, that there is no reality, only texts. If there is something other than nonsense and trivialities, I haven't found it. But it is very useful. It intimidates young people, it is good for your career and it allows you to pose as being more radical than the rest while you basically remove yourself from any form of struggle. There are good and serious people involved in this, but as a generalization, I think that what I'm telling you is accurate.

HD: Have you written anything about this?

NC: Only when they drag me toward it. I've been under a lot of pressure to discuss these issues because they have caused a great deal of hysteria within the left. I have participated in an exchange on rationality and post-modernism. But I try not to waste my time on these things.

9

The Global Society

In a new era, we foresee that our military power will remain an essential underpinning of the global balance, but less prominently and in different ways... The growing technological sophistication of Third World conflicts will place serious demands on our forces [and may] continue to threaten U.S. interests [even without] the backdrop of superpower competition.

National Security Strategy report, 1990[1]

Throughout the Cold War, we contained a global threat to market democracies: now we should seek to enlarge their reach.

Anthony Lake, National Security adviser, 1990[2]

Heinz Dieterich: What's your opinion of the concept of the "global society"?

Noam Chomsky: Basically, it's a term that doesn't make much sense. If you analyze phenomena like the flow of investment capital across borders in accordance with the capacity of the economies, then the global society isn't very different from what there was at the beginning of the century. Of course, there have been great

---

* This interview was conducted in March 1996.

changes in the social order and, in this sense, the term is not so bad. But, we do need to use it carefully.

Even though the large transnationals now control an extraordinary part of the global economy, they are very dependent on their own states. One of the best recent studies of the 100 most important transnationals on the *Fortune* list found that all of them had benefited from specific interventions by the nation states where they are based.

Of the 100, 20 had been rescued from total collapse by state intervention, which means that they have been very dependent on the government and on the subsidies they receive from the population of their own nation state. Take the United States, for example, where there is the largest number of transnationals. They all depend on things like public subsidies which they receive through the Pentagon system and other sources. We would not have many large corporations if it wasn't for public financing and public financing comes from taxpayer contributions. And if businesses get into trouble, it's charged to the U.S. taxpayers' account. The same is true of British and Japanese transnationals.

Large corporations are taking over more and more sectors of the economy, which is similar to that which occurred in the early days of modern industrialization in 18th century England. There is a market, but it is a market guided by the state, and the nanny state is a crucial factor upon which all corporations depend. Obviously, there are also differences. There is, for example, a large expansion of finance capital, and the portion of the pie that belongs to it is much larger than before. It has become dominant in relation to industrial capital and this has significant effects.

Take, for example, foreign direct investment in Latin America. They are calling Latin America one of the big emerging markets and everyone is excited. But, available data on foreign direct investment by the United States in Latin America in 1994 reveals that the largest part, some 25 percent of it, goes to the Bermudas.

Does this mean that they are moving factories to the Bermudas? No, they go because it's a tax haven; it's probably used for drug running and who knows what else. That's why the U.S. banks go there. If you add another haven for these kinds of financial transactions, like the Cayman Islands, then it's closer to 50 percent of foreign direct investment. They're not small numbers.

It's similar to what happened in Mexico. A huge quantity of money entered during the period of the so-called economic miracle, but as everybody seemed to know, except the economists of the World Bank, they were portfolio investments, non-productive funds that can leave as quickly as they came.

HD: So can we continue to meaningfully use the term "global society"?

NC: I think we can use it as long as we don't confuse its meaning. It is, without doubt, a significant phenomenon. For example, the sales of the foreign branches of the transnationals exceed considerably the value of all exports. If you look at what they call "trade," you can see why all that rhetoric about markets and GATT is a complete fraud. Around 40 percent of U.S. trade consists of the internal trade of U.S. corporations. This means, for example, that Ford sends something from Michigan to its northern Mexico assembly plants and then returns it to Michigan, because that way they make bigger profits. And they call that "exports to Mexico" and "imports to the United States." Well, this makes up close to half of our "trade." So, when NAFTA was signed, more that half of U.S. "exports" never entered the Mexican market — it was simply internal trade. All these operations are part of the internal functioning of large totalitarian institutions, which are basically huge economies centrally planned by very visible hands. There is no invisible hand there.

Corporations set themselves up to violate the discipline of the market. That is their reason for being. They must internalize the risk, they have a centralized command, they are big and they have a devastating effect on world trade. The figures are huge. And this is only part of the problem. Billions of dollars are shifted every day from one financial market to another by the large financial institutions, always in pursuit of the same goals: lower growth rates, reduced wages and increased profits.

These are important phenomena. And it's not that they can't be controlled. They are simply specific social and economic policies that could be changed, not laws of the market or anything like that.

HD: Is there a principle of development or of historical progress or is it only the sum of individual chaotic actions?

NC: I think there is a general principle that, outside of a few small areas of the natural sciences, our knowledge is not very deep and remains on a superficial level. Therefore, when people give complicated descriptions of things, they are probably doing it because of their careers or something like that.

Take the question you're asking. If you examine history, there have certainly been changes, and there are some circumstances which make those recognizable. For example, if you compare the society of the 17th century with the current one, there's certainly much more freedom today almost everywhere. They no longer quarter you and throw you in a pit for criticizing the state, as happened in 18th century England. There's no feudalism and there's no slavery, at least not in the United States. After World War I, women were formally allowed to participate in the political system. During the last 30 years there has at least been the beginning of an acknowledgment — even though in practice nothing is done to make amends — of the original sin of U.S. society, namely, the annihilation of the native population. Before then, this was not even acknowledged.

Looking back over a long period of history and speaking in generalities, one could probably say that there was a broadening of the scope of freedom and justice. But, on the other hand, there is a whole range of competing tendencies. For example, there is a big tendency towards the expansion of totalitarianism. Corporations are totalitarian institutions. In fact, they originated from the same intellectual breeding-ground as Bolshevism and fascism, from nineteenth century Hegelian ideas about social organizations with rights over the individual. From that developed various contemporary forms of totalitarianism. Bolshevism and fascism have basically ceased to exist, but the corporation is flowering and spreading. Therefore, what they call the triumph of the market is, in fact, the triumph of totalitarianism.

Corporations are totalitarian institutions with a centralized command, combining executive, legislative and judicial functions in one unit. And they have a deep commitment to propaganda and mind control. For example, one seventh of U.S. Gross Domestic Product — around a billion dollars per year — is spent on public relations and marketing, which basically represent different forms of manipulation and deceit. The scale of this is massive. The 500 most important transnational companies listed in *Fortune* magazine control around two-thirds of U.S. Gross Domestic Product and a huge part of the international economy. They are all connected with each other and, as a result, the net is even tighter. This is a burden that weighs on the market and, of course, on democracy. We can observe, therefore, that there are tendencies which evolve in very different directions.

Of course, one can formulate this in another type of language —

for example, in a language that refers to Hegel or to Hegelian latecomers of the Fukuyama type — but then, I think, it basically becomes ridiculous. These people take simple things that are not very well understood and, through elaborate language, make them come across as something very complicated.

HD: Do the ideals of the enlightenment and liberalism remain valid?

NC: I believe that the ideals of the enlightenment have a lot of validity and must be taken very seriously. Of course, we are not in the 18th century. Everything is different and those values have to be adapted to contemporary circumstances. The forms of thought that inspired people like von Humboldt, Adam Smith and the founders of Manchester liberalism are pre-capitalist. We can't really say that they are anti-capitalist in their convictions. And, in a certain sense, in fact, their ideals were crushed against the rocks of capitalism which destroyed classical liberalism and the ideals of the enlightenment

Those ideals must be taken very seriously. They recur in popular struggles. If you read, for example, the working class literature of the 19th century from the Boston area, which was the center of the U.S. industrial revolution, you'll find a literature that revolves around an industrial democracy of the libertarian-socialist, anarchist, radical type. They considered the growth of industrial capitalism to be an attack on the rights they'd won in the revolution. And that was absolutely correct. They attacked the degradation of the worker who was subjected not only to the command of the machine, but also to the command of the bosses. And this comes directly from Adam Smith.

HD: The Zapatista movement organizes continental congresses "against neoliberalism and for humanity" in order to build a worldwide program for democratic change. You are one of the few people with the knowledge to develop such a program. Would you participate in this?

NC: Yes, of course. For the greater part of my life I have done so. Because I might be too busy, I would probably not be physically where the event takes place, but these are precisely the kind of things that have to be done. There is a huge number of people in the world — probably the vast majority — that is strongly opposed to the economic and social policies being carried out on a global scale.

Those policies are called "neoliberal," but it should be recognized that there is a lot of fraud in that. They are neoliberal programs for the victims, but not for the manipulators. The United States is a good example. The people who try to impose the principles of neoliberalism in the Third World and in the slums of our cities don't want the same principles for themselves. They want a powerful nanny state to protect them, as always. That is why the media, intellectuals and economists have to make out that they don't understand this; that's part of their work.

Take, for example, the Pentagon budget. For years, the fairy tale about this budget was that it protected us from "the Russians." That's why we needed a big budget for the Pentagon. But now there are no more "Russians." So, what happens with the Pentagon budget? It remains the same. Taxes rise under the impetus of people who call themselves "conservatives." The ultra-right Heritage Foundation, which provides the basic thinking for Congress, as well as Newt Gingrich and others, demand an increase in the Pentagon budget for reasons that the business world has always understood only too well.

The Pentagon budget has a domestic function. It ensures that the rich and privileged are protected from the discipline of the market. When I mention the Pentagon budget, I'm not only talking about the military's funds, I'm talking about the whole system, including NASA, the Energy Department and, for now, the National Health Institutes. All of these institutions are basically domestic mechanisms for the transfer of public funds to the advanced sectors of industry.

This is the reason why the Pentagon budget continues to stay high. If Newt Gingrich's clientele wants to stay rich, it must avoid the discipline of the market. If it had to face the discipline of the market, it would be selling rags. So, markets are good for seven-year-old children in the slums of New York, for the people of Mexico City and the mountains, but not for the rich. This not only isn't neoliberalism, it's what you could call the really-existing market doctrine, which comes from the earliest days of the industrial revolution.

HD: Are tensions among the United States, China and Taiwan, the United States–Cuba conflict, and the problems in Palestine–Israel manifestations of the New World Order?

NC: In fact, they are three different cases. The current friction between the United States and China is reminiscent of a sparring match. On the one hand, since the time of Nixon the United States has recognized that the island is part of China. But on the other, it wants to keep Taiwan outside China. The Chinese also have an ambiguous position towards this problem. Officially, the Chinese government considers Taiwan part of China, but it understands that there is no way of incorporating it into China. There is a good dose of military maneuvering and ostentation around this. Frankly, I don't think that it will explode into a major conflict, but the situation is undoubtedly tense.

The reaction to Cuba's downing of two light planes [in February 1996] is another example of fraud perpetrated by the intellectual community. For 30 years, the United States has carried out terrorist warfare against Cuba, blowing up factories and applying a very severe embargo, because we had to defend ourselves from "the Russian threat."

There's no longer a Russian threat. So, what happens? The United States extends its attacks on Cuba. This tells you exactly how significant the Russian threat was, the same way the Pentagon budget tells you how worried they were about the Russians. At any rate, Cuba now seems more vulnerable and therefore the United States intensifies its attacks.

Turning to the current problems. Of course Cuba shouldn't be downing planes. But ask yourself, what would happen if Libyan planes flew over New York dropping leaflets, calling on people to overthrow the government and, probably, throwing down instructions on how to blow up a building. What would happen? Well, we don't need to ask. We can simply move on to the Palestine–Israel issue.

Israel doesn't down planes, because no one goes there. But it does sink boats. Israel has carried out terrorism in international waters for years. It attacks ferries that travel from Cyprus to Beirut, sometimes sinking them. It has killed people in the water, kidnapped people traveling on ships and jailed them for 20 years without any charges being laid. This is public knowledge.

Has anything done by Cuba come even remotely close to this? No. Does anyone care about Israel's activities? No. This means that anyone who screams about what the Cubans have done can't be taken seriously even for a second. It's like asking Hitler if he was against the killing of human beings. The collection of politicians gathered at the international terrorism conference in Egypt last week consisted of the biggest terrorists around. The fact that they can meet as anti-terrorists without causing ridicule or anger is truly amazing.

U.S. policy on Cuba is at a turning point. There's a sort of balance. The business community is no longer keen on the blockade, but there are other forces that want to make sure that no one adopts the Cuban's bad ideas.

While this whole scandal about Cuba was going on, the government of South Africa accepted a new group of Cuban doctors who had gone to work in rural areas. President Mandela and others complimented Cuba for its solidarity and support. At that moment, Cuba probably had more doctors working in rural areas than the rest of the world put together — it certainly had more than any other country. That's the type of thing that worries the United States. The poor of South Africa received the Cubans with affection, as you can imagine. But this didn't appear in the news here. The news agencies didn't cover it.

Those are the things that have always worried the United States, because they send the wrong message, that independence is possible, that a country can work to resolve its domestic problems rather than for a foreign master, and so on. This is the dangerous message. Everyone must know that the people who send that message will be seriously hurt, not only must they be sent out of business but they should be struck hard, in Mafia Don style. If someone doesn't pay protection money, you don't only take their money, you punish them as well.

On the other hand, U.S. corporations want to go to Cuba and steal. And now that they see that Cuba might collapse, they want to participate and ensure that everything doesn't end up in the hands of the Japanese and the Europeans. So there's a conflict similar to the one that occurred over Vietnam and this is reflected in the country's foreign policy.

Let's go to the Israel–Palestine problem. What's happened is pretty amazing. For approximately 25 years, the United States has been virtually alone with Israel, against the whole world, insisting on a rejectionist position with regard to UN Resolution 242, which demands the withdrawal of Israel from the Occupied Territories. The United States has opposed this resolution since 1971, and from 1976 had to veto Security Council resolutions and vote in the General Assembly against (near-unanimous) resolutions calling for Palestinian self-determination, also blocking initiatives from all other parties.

Finally, following the Gulf War, the rest of the world became sufficiently intimidated for the United States to impose its own rejectionist program. And it did so. First at the Madrid negotiations, then at Oslo I and Oslo II. Oslo II institutionalizes a system that is worse than the one established by South Africa when they institutionalized apartheid. And the apartheid government also called those small territories they established "states," such as, for example, Transkei. In fact, this simply reflects the positions of the leaders of the rejectionist front, led by the United States. It's a tremendous victory for the rule of force and also a tremendous victory for the propaganda regime. Our propaganda regime is accepted not only by Europe, which isn't overly surprising, but now even by the Third World as well. This is a significant change compared with the situation just five years ago. In summary, it's as if Syria had conquered the territory and allowed the Jews to direct the traffic in Tel Aviv, with the Syrian troops managing everything else.

HD: Some of Cuba's main leaders read your essays and liked them a lot. Does this surprise you?

NC: [Laughing] No, not at all.

HD: If they invited you, would you go and under what conditions?

NC: I would be perfectly prepared to go, but I've got the usual problem of time. This is partly a result of the fact that intellectuals have sold out almost completely in the last 20 to 30 years, so there's almost no one around. At the same time, there's a big increase in grassroots activism. And, as a result, the requests for participation, information and talks are simply overwhelming.

Currently, Pat Buchanan travels the country with his right-wing version of the slogans of Students for a Democratic Society of the 1960s and, just imagine, talks to the workers. Also, a magazine called *Socialist Review* has just come out. It's the most recent incarnation of one of the great new left magazines of the 1960s. You know what it's dedicated to? Queer history.

Aside from the importance that this could have, it tells you something when *Socialist Review* is dedicated to queer history, while someone like Buchanan appropriates the slogans of the left.

Unfortunately, that's the situation in this country and in the world. When you go to Third World countries and you talk about Western intellectuals, almost certainly everyone is up on the latest version of deconstructionism. Just what the people need.

10

Mexico:
Between NAFTA
and the Zapatistas

... it is clear that order depends on somehow compelling the newly mobilized strata to return to a measure of passivity and defeatism.

Ithiel Pool, Massachusetts Institute of Technology[1]

You have the freedom here to do what you want to do with your money, and to me, that is worth all the political freedom in the world.

U.S. banker commenting on Venezuela under the
Pérez Jiménez dictatorship[2]

Following World War II the United States assumed, out of self-interest, responsibility for the welfare of the world capitalist system.

Gerald Haines, senior historian of the CIA,
The Americanization of Brazil, 1989

---

* This interview was conducted in January 1997.

Heinz Dieterich: What effects has NAFTA had for Mexico and the United States, and for the rich and the poor?
Noam Chomsky: I think it's important to distinguish the United States and Mexico from the rich and the poor which, of course, are categories that crosscut the United States and Mexico. It's also important to distinguish between what has happened since the passing of NAFTA and the effect of NAFTA, which is something very different.

We can discover what's happened since the passage of NAFTA. It's been very beneficial for the rich in both countries and very harmful to the poor in both countries. In the United States, probably hundreds of thousands of reasonably well-paying jobs have been lost as transnationals have simply shifted operations to Mexico where they can get far cheaper and more suppressed labor. That's not a benefit to Mexico which has also lost millions of jobs because the productive apparatus collapsed — as of course was going to happen. The point of forcing them to open up the barriers was to allow them to be taken over by transnationals that export to foreign markets, obviously they aren't going to be able to sustain that. In fact, the Mexican Chamber of Commerce predicted that and it now reports that more than half of businesses have suffered, but mainly smaller businesses. The associates of the big transnationals are doing fine. Mexico is exporting to the United States, but that's not because export industry has increased. It's because the domestic market has collapsed.

There's no need to talk about the effects on Mexican society. Probably about half the population can barely get enough food to survive, while the man who controls the corn market is still on the list of billionaires which is the one category in Mexico that ranks pretty high. And that's, I think, the general picture and it's not at all surprising. It was largely predictable.

How much of this is the effect of NAFTA? Well, that's hard to say because you'd have to ask how much NAFTA changed anything, and that's a difficult question. I think the answer appears to be that it didn't change anything very much. These were processes that were underway. Maybe NAFTA accelerated them slightly, but it's not easy to put a measure on it.

Incidentally, it is now openly conceded by advocates of NAFTA that what they were claiming was a complete fraud. There was all sorts of talk about the wonderful effects it would have on Mexico and the United States, and how it would improve the economy and jobs and so on — read *Foreign Affairs* for example. It's now recognized that that was a fraud — that what the critics were saying was correct and that, as they now put it, and indeed then put it, the purpose of NAFTA was to lock Mexico into the so-called "reforms." So, if there ever is what was called a "democracy opening" in Mexico — that great threat that maybe it'll become more democratic — there wouldn't be much that could be done because the economic policies that subordinate Mexico to U.S.-based transnational capital would be locked in place by a treaty. That was pretty obvious before and it is now publicly conceded. At a Latin American strategy development conference at the Pentagon in around 1990, it was concluded that at that time relations with Mexico were fine, but that there was a danger that a "democracy opening," as they put it, might bring about a Mexican government more committed to nationalist and populist goals. The main purpose of NAFTA was to block that threat of a democracy opening and to lock Mexico in by treaty arrangements and that's probably been done. The terrible effects for much of the population are partially a consequence of this, but partially they're just a continuation of other processes and it's kind of hard to sort them out and say this is due to NAFTA.

HD: The second trade bloc in the Americas is the Mercosur. What's your guess about the development of these blocs? Are they rivals? Will they join in the future?

NC: We know what the goals of the various contestants are and it's not obvious how they're going to sort themselves out. Since the colonial period, one of the big problems with Latin America has been that relations among the countries, even among regions within the countries, have largely been broken and they have individually been related to, and hence dependent on, foreign imperial powers.

The breakdown of internal relations in Latin America took place under Spanish colonialism, then under English influence, and in recent years U.S. influence, but connections among the countries are slight and even connections among the regions tend to be slight. The United States would, of course, like to maintain that.

Of course, the United States is not the only player in the game at this point. Europe is reconstructing some of its lost influence and relations with Latin America, and Japan is now one of the leading suppliers of investment funds and development aid. So it's a complicated arrangement.

The United States would certainly like the Mercosur to be subordinated to the same highly protectionist trade system that it's managed to establish in North America (NAFTA).

It's an issue among the South American countries and they're not insignificant in scale. There's considerable internal conflict as to whether they should adapt themselves to these arrangements, or move towards policies that are more oriented towards the needs of the domestic population. Again, we have to go back to the distinction between rich and poor and not the distinction between countries. Some sectors in Latin American society are oriented towards transnational capital and want to be local associates of transnational capital — they will probably want [the trade agreement] to be incorporated within the U.S.-dominated, rather highly protectionist, trading system. Other sectors have different goals and I don't think you can make predictions any more than you can predict the outcome of the social conflicts that are very visible all through South America.

HD: The U.S. government says that Mexico is an issue of national security for the United States. What does that mean? What are the implications of such a statement?

NC: The best comment on that was made by a Mexican diplomat about 30 years ago, when Kennedy was trying to get Mexico to join U.S. actions against Cuba on the grounds that Cuba was a threat to U.S. national security. He's alleged to have said that Mexico couldn't join, because if Mexico were to pretend that Cuba was a threat to its security, 40 million Mexicans would die laughing. It's approximately the same in this case. There's nothing that can conceivably be an issue of national security.

The last conflict between the United States and Mexico was when the United States conquered one third of Mexico and took it over and it's now the American south west. The issue of "national security" is about security for U.S. investors. They have problems with security. They want to make sure that they can continue to profit from speculation in Mexico through what's very misleadingly called "trade" — that is, extending their operations to Mexico to make use of highly exploited labor and freedom from environmental regulations and then shipping parts back to the United States. None of that is trade in any meaningful sense, but they'd like to continue to exploit that, and if there is what they fear — a democracy opening in Mexico — it could threaten those arrangements. Those are the only security issues.

HD: How does the U.S. government and public opinion in the United States see the Zapatista movement after two years? What about movements like EPR?

NC: The U.S. government would certainly like to see them suppressed and would be happy to see them suppressed by violence if possible. Right after the Zapatistas came into the public eye, they were able to gain a good deal of public exposure both in Mexico and even beyond in very imaginative ways, and that protected them. That made it hard for the Mexican government, surely with U.S. support, to just move in and violently destroy them. Since then, there's been an attempt to remove them from the public eye so that such measures can be undertaken and, in the United States at least, it's probably more or less successful. I don't think many people are aware of the Zapatistas at this point. The EPR nobody knows about; there's only a few reports now and then. It's very important to maintain and, indeed, extend public concern and commitment because that's the main protection that any popular movement has against destruction. I myself can't comment on the EPR — I don't know anything about it and I don't understand what it is. The Zapatistas are better understood and it's very important to maintain and extend public attention and concern because that's the principal protection which a popular movement has against destruction.

HD: But they are not seen as a threat to U.S. investments? Are U.S. investors worried about the Zapatistas any more?

NC: What they're worried about is any kind of conflict within Mexico — labor organizing, for example — anything that threatens what they call "stability," which means rigid control of the sectors of the population that are subordinate to their interests. Anything that threatens that, of course, is a threat to security. A "democracy opening" is a threat. Any kind of popular movement would be a threat. Nationalist policies on the part of Mexican business would be a threat. Anything that makes Mexico something other than a service area for private power is a threat.

HD: In light of globalization, are national liberation projects such as that pursued by the Colombian liberation movement still viable, or are such struggles a thing of the past?

NC: National liberation is always viable. The guerrilla movements were a meaningful contribution to national liberation in so far as they had significant social roots. If they were an expression of popular struggle which turned to a guerrilla conflict in response to the unwillingness of the powerful to allow the expansion of social justice and human rights — if that's what they were — yes, they were viable. To a large extent they lost those roots, I think. The situation in Colombia is kind of complicated. Doubtless the FARC does have ties with elements of Colombian peasant society, but it's a pretty complicated story.

In Central America, the groups basically no longer exist because of the effectiveness of state terror in demolishing their popular base. They may have some viability within the political system — that's important and I think they do — but what's necessary is to sustain and rebuild the civil society that was devastated by a decade of terror. That has its effects. The effects were well described by a Jesuit conference in San Salvador a couple of years ago, which pointed out that one should not overlook the long-term effects of what they called the "culture of terror." The effects are, as they put it, to "domesticate the aspirations of the majority" who are no longer willing to even think about options that don't conform to the needs of the powerful. Well, to a certain extent that's happened and unless the aspirations of the majority break free from such domestication, popular movements won't develop. Whether popular movements lead to guerrilla struggle, I think, depends on the violence of the powerful. If they reject the demands for social justice, freedom and human rights and if state repression mounts, people may defend themselves. But the kind of say, *foco*, strategy that was talked about years ago... I never thought it made any sense, and I don't think it's viable today.

HD: Do you see a regional Latin American project as viable?

NC: It's viable, but the main problems in Latin America today are really internal. The states are subordinated to their wealthy classes to an extent that is beyond the norm throughout the world. It happens everywhere, of course, but it's well beyond the norm in Latin America where the wealthy simply don't have social obligations and state power is subordinated to them. Until that internal problem is overcome, they don't have any chance either to use their own resources for their own welfare, or to carry out any regional projects. But, in my opinion, the fact that it's substantially an internal problem is rather hopeful because it means it can be overcome. Sure, there are pressures from the outside and often pretty ugly ones. But there are plenty of opportunities, particularly in South America, where there's plenty of wealth and resources. Countries like Brazil and Argentina and Chile have lots of options open to them, if they can put their internal houses in order.

HD: It seems that there is growing evidence that the United States and national elites are once again mounting a continental state terror network as they did in the 1970s. Have you noticed anything like that?

NC: I don't think it would be very surprising, but I don't think there's much evidence for it, at least that I know of. Undoubtedly it's true in countries like Colombia where there is very large-scale state terror and the United States has certainly been heavily involved in that. Colombia has been one of the major recipients of U.S. military aid and training through the early 1990s. Whether it's continent-wide, I don't know and I'm a bit skeptical. I don't think that conditions are such that it would be an appropriate response at this point. I think the United States and the national oligarchies are expecting or hoping that this neoliberal stranglehold will have the effect of subordinating the populations to domestic and foreign capital. Maybe that'll work, maybe not. If it doesn't work, then I would expect a revival of state terror.

Incidentally, I think that the possibilities for state terror are probably much less than they were 30 years ago. There have been changes. So, the chances of a military coup, or of direct U.S. involvement in a military coup, have, I think, declined. In part, because the world is just more complex. The United States is no longer the overwhelmingly dominant actor that it was 30 years ago and, for internal reasons, it's not in a position to openly and publicly support state terror and military coups the way it did, say, in the Kennedy–Johnson years.

HD: In his latest book, [Caspar] Weinberger[3] says something about the possibility of a U.S. military intervention in the next decade if things go wrong in Mexico. Is that just fantasy?

NC: Right now it's not worth thinking about what'll happen in 10 years — who knows? No, I don't think it's anything that deserves much consideration.

HD: If the European Union made a cooperation agreement with Mexico as well as with Cuba (contingent upon human rights improvements and so on), would we then have two world powers dictating policy in Latin America?

NC: Notice that the European Union is talking primarily about Cuba and partially about Mexico. They're not talking about Indonesia, they're not talking about Colombia, they're not talking about Saudi Arabia. They're perfectly happy to cooperate with them, however vicious and violent they are. That's a reflection of their subordination to U.S. power. These are U.S. priorities. The

United States is perfectly happy to have violent state power and repression in Indonesia and Saudi Arabia. It wants to recover its traditional control over Cuba and it wants to ensure that Mexico remains in the U.S. framework. Europe, while to some extent pursuing an independent course, has certainly not freed itself from U.S. dominance.

We can put aside the discussion about human rights improvement and free elections. That is transparently a fraud, as we see when we look at cases where those concerns are expressed and compare them with the often much worse cases where they're not expressed. So that's a fraud — we can put it aside. It's a doctrinal matter. The real issue that arises in this connection is the relationship between the European Union and the United States. Well, the EU states are making exploratory steps toward developing an independent position in the world. But they surely recognize the overwhelming economic and military power of the United States and they're unwilling to confront it. There are plenty of conflicts within Europe about this. France, for example, takes a different position from England. And how those will be resolved, you can't tell.

There's a third major bloc that has to be considered in this respect, namely, the Japan-based bloc — and the interplay among those countries has been of no small significance in the past 20 or 30 years. The dictates of Latin American policy have to be resolved by Latin Americans themselves. Again, that's mainly an internal problem.

South America, in particular, is not Central Africa — they have plenty of options. Of course, they're relatively weak in comparison to the major powers, but not powerless by any means. If they can deal with their internal problems, I think they have a lot of opportunities to resist dictation of policy from anywhere.

HD: Do the Latin American elites lack the political will to unite and confront that problem?

NC: No, they have plenty of political will to enrich themselves and to use states as instruments for their own power. That's been their traditional role and they want to maintain it.

HD: So they don't want to confront the foreign allies?

NC: Why should they? Go back to India under the British Empire. Indian elites were for the most part quite happy, in fact very pro-imperial — they were enriching themselves. There were nationalist elements, especially later on. But throughout most of the British imperial era, the elite elements were quite supportive of the Empire. Same in Latin America. They sometimes want to get more control for themselves. But they achieve their elite position by association with foreign power, and they're not interested in breaking those relations.

11

The Pope, Cuba
and the Asian Crisis

Underlying the popular sentiment, which might have evaporated in time, which forced the United States to take up arms against Spanish rule in Cuba, were our economic relations with the West Indies and the South American republics. So strong was this commercial instinct that had there been no emotional cause, such as the alleged enormities of Spanish rule or the destruction of the Maine, we would have doubtless taken steps in the end to abate with a strong hand what seemed to be an economic nuisance... The Spanish-American War was but an incident of a general movement of expansion which had its root in the changed environment of an industrial capacity far beyond our domestic powers of consumption. It was seen to be necessary for us not only to find foreign purchasers for our goods, but to provide the means of making access to foreign markets easy, economical and safe.

Chief of the bureau of foreign commerce
at the U.S. Commerce Department, 1902[1]

* This interview was conducted in January 1998.

Heinz Dieterich: The first question is about the Pope's trip to Cuba. In terms of this visit, what are Cuba's interests and what are the Pope's interests?

Noam Chomsky: Well, Cuba is clearly interested in becoming more integrated into world society and escaping the exclusion imposed by the United States. As for the Pope, it's hard to say. He may be trying to compensate for the role that he has played in helping to undermine much of the progressive church in Latin America, or he may see this as another move towards continuing that enterprise. It's rather hard to know.

HD: In 1898, the United States sent the battleship *Maine* to Havana; in 1998 the Pope goes there. Who's the more dangerous of the two?

NC: The sinking of the battleship *Maine* was the pretext for the U.S. intervention which essentially terminated the liberation war [which the Cubans were waging against the Spanish] and turned Cuba into a U.S. colony. We know what that led to. The interaction with the Pope is, I think, uncertain. It could mean many things. The most positive interpretation or hope is that it could offer more opportunities for Cuba to escape the strangulation imposed by the U.S. embargo and continuing terror.

HD: So past experience is no guide — what the Pope tried to do in Nicaragua is no indication?

NC: It's very hard to say. The agenda that the Pope pursued not only in Nicaragua, but even more dramatically in Brazil and then El Salvador, and elsewhere, has been to undermine the preferential option for the poor in the Church, which was such an extraordinarily powerful force. It was countered with extreme violence, and the Vatican's role was not helpful, to put it mildly. On the other hand, the Pope has also taken a stand against the savagery and inhumanity of the neoliberal version of state capitalism and the way it's being imposed on the Third World, and what it's leading to. There still remain conflicting elements within the church and I don't think it's possible to predict the outcome. I think it will depend a lot on what happens at the local level — just as in the case of the rise of liberation theology in the 1960s and 1970s. It was largely a reflection of things that were happening at the grassroots level.

HD: Why did the United States not try to annex Cuba at the end of the liberation war as had happened with Puerto Rico, Hawaii and Guam?

NC: Remember, they didn't literally annex any of those places. Hawaii wasn't technically annexed and didn't become a state until the 1950s. Guam was taken as a protectorate and kept that way (in opposition to the general structure of the world system after World War II). Puerto Rico remains a dependency, but not technically annexed. For U.S. investors, it was a good decision in terms of profit to allow Cuba a nominal form of independence under U.S. domination. It was turned into a kind of a plantation and later a gambling center and a tourist center and so on.

There are various techniques of control and direct annexation is by no means the most efficient. The period in which Europe — and, of course, the United States is an extension of it — literally took over the colonies and ran them from the metropolis was mainly the late 19th century. By the early 20th century, it was mostly eroding throughout the world and other forms of domination, often more efficient ones, were replacing it. Even in the days of colonial control, it was a mixed system. For example, when the British ran India, technically it was run from London, but in fact it was largely administered by Indians.

HD: Does the death of [CANF leader] Mas Canosa open new possibilities, or is it of only marginal importance?

NC: The question really is what the effect will be within the Cuban community, mainly in Florida and a few other places. Will it lead to the development of other tendencies within that community that might help move things toward a more productive, constructive relationship with Cuba and weaken the intense and rather violent pressures that have come from that community under Mas Canosa's leadership?

I think that it's by no means definite which direction U.S. policy will take. Strong elements of U.S. business are in favor of an opening to Cuba, which would essentially reintegrate it within the U.S. system, but in the manner of other semi-independent areas. So, for example, when Castro was in New York, he was greeted by a group of businessmen led by David Rockefeller.

The same kind of thing happened in the case of Vietnam. In fact, in the 1950s there was a serious split in U.S. policy as to what attitude it ought to take towards China. Should it take an attitude of extreme hostility, driving China into the hands of the Soviet Union, knowing, of course, that there was a serious conflict between them? Or, should it adopt essentially the policy that was later taken by Nixon and Kissinger, who integrated China into the U.S.-dominated system while leaving it with a degree of independence and autonomy? Those are tactical choices. It can go either way.

Take an even more dramatic case. In the late 1940s, the CIA intelligence analyses identified Bolivia and Guatemala as the two major threats to U.S. interests — meaning U.S. domination in the hemisphere — because both had what they called "radical nationalist movements." The United States took opposite stands in those two cases. In the case of Guatemala, it moved to overthrow the government with a military coup. In the case of Bolivia, where the government was more radical — Trotskyite-led and radical miners and so on — it took the opposite stand. It integrated them into the U.S. system. The end result is not too different in the two cases; the United States simply made opposite tactical choices in somewhat similar situations. It could have gone the other way.

These are tactical decisions based on tentative and uncertain judgments. The goals are fairly clear, but there are many ways of realizing them. The hawkish way is to try to realize them by force. The dovish way is to realize them by the use of overwhelming financial and economic power and inducements that will incorporate them within the system in other ways. And if you look through the history of certainly the last 50 years, but in fact all history of European expansion over the world, it's taken many forms. Japan was never conquered, but it could have been.

HD: So, one possibility for Cuba is that it will go the way Vietnam has?

NC: Well, that's one prospect, but there are others. Third World solidarity and people to people solidarity between the First and the Third World could allow space for a very different set of developments throughout the Third World altogether. Remember, these divisions are not based on colors on maps. The richest and most powerful country in the world is the United States. But a substantial part of the population, in fact by some criteria a majority of the population, really faces problems not unlike those of the Third World — diminishing incomes, loss of security of work, and so on. These are problems that have been growing in the past 20 years particularly in the Anglo-American societies, but also throughout the rich countries, as the world system gradually changes. Policies which resemble structural adjustment are implemented within the rich countries as well. So American workers and Mexican workers are at last recognizing common interests which they indeed have.

HD: And what does the Asian crisis mean for Cuba and other poor countries — for people?

NC: That depends very much how the Asian crisis is resolved. The IMF and other international financial institutions, along with the United States and other major European powers, may try to bring about a kind of Latin Americanization of East Asia. That is, to further open the economies to essentially foreign takeovers, to allow free capital flow, free financial flows. Such conditions have existed for a long time in Latin America, which is part of their problem. In fact, to a certain extent, they've already been extended to East Asia and that's a large part of the problem behind the crisis.

But, the East Asian countries do have the possibility of resisting that and may do so. I think that's an unpredictable conflict shaping up right in front of our eyes. If East Asia is indeed Latin Americanized, then I think the prospects for the other countries of the South are diminished. On the other hand, if it can be sustained as a more or less independent, developing region and can be democratized, as has been happening in South Korea at least, well that could be a more positive development.

HD: Has the Asian crisis had an impact at the ideological level on the notion of the infallibility of capitalist development which has been preached for the last 10 to 15 years?

NC: This a question of the extent to which people are capable of penetrating beyond the ideological doctrines and looking at the facts. There was a significant change in world order in the early 1970s. The post-World War II system, the so-called Bretton Woods system, was based on the principle that capital flows should be regulated and trade should be liberalized. It was understood by [the economist, John Maynard] Keynes and the American negotiator, Harry Dexter White, and others, that financial liberalization and trade liberalization quite often run counter to one another. They were hoping to develop what was sometimes called an "embedded form of liberalism" in which there would be free trade, regulation of financial flows and some kind of social contract internally — a welfare state — at least for the rich countries. That was the system.

Well, starting a little bit in the late 1960s, but dramatically in the 1970s, that system broke down. Or rather, it was broken down. The United States and England, joined occasionally by others, simply broke the system down and moved towards liberalization of financial flows. There was deregulation of capital flows. And since then, there has been increased market volatility, with increasing crises — ups and downs, violent swings and so on.

It has also been a period of restriction of trade. This is considered a period of free trade, but that's not true. In fact, the Reagan administration was dramatically protectionist. Meanwhile, the liberalization of capital flows has gradually extended over the world — Europe dropped its capital controls (mostly continental Europe in the 1980s), the East Asian countries and South Korea just very recently. So it has been a period of increasing and unpredictable crises and rapid oscillations from highs to lows, also a period of lower growth. World growth cut back in the 1970s, 1980s and 1990s as compared with what it had been in the past.

There has also been a period of increasing inequality. So, in the United States, for about 80 percent of the population incomes have either stagnated or declined over 20 years, while there has been enormous concentration of wealth at the higher sectors (the top two percent).

It has been a period in which the value of assets has separated from the value of the real economy in a very dramatic fashion. So, up until say around the mid 1980s, if you looked at it over a long period, the value of stocks on Wall Street was pretty well correlated with the actual wealth of the country, with the Gross National Product. In the mid-1980s, they separated sharply and there has been what's called "asset inflation," radical asset inflation. The money value of stocks on the market is by now radically uncorrelated with the actual wealth produced by the economy and nobody knows where that's going to lead — could lead to another disaster. There has also been an astronomical increase in speculative financial flows. They've gone totally out of sight since the early 1970s and they are also largely unrelated to the real economy.

Globalization, as it's called these days, is not very different from what it was before World War II, when measured by trade, investment flows, so on and so forth. Relative to the economy it's about what it was before World War I. On the other hand, at that time and up until the 1970s, international financial flows were overwhelmingly related to the real economy, that is, they had to do with investment and trade. But now, about maybe five or 10 percent is related to investment and trade and the rest is speculative. In fact, a substantial part of foreign investment is actually just takeovers or manipulations, not productive investment. These are big changes, and they have led to volatility, uncertainty, unpredictable crises and bailouts. Take, say, the current Asian crisis. The total bailout so far is in the order of roughly $100 billion. The S&L [Savings and Loan] crisis in the United States, which is just a trivial part of the U.S. economy, is worth over $200 billion, just a few years ago. Just to put some scale on these things.

HD: Sometimes I've had the feeling that there is a change in, let's say, the mental climate, the psychological climate, that reminds me sometimes of the 1960s — students are beginning to organize and protest again. Have you had that feeling too or am I wrong?

NC: For one thing, it never really stopped. The image that's presented — let's just keep to the United States — is that in the 1960s there was a great deal of ferment and then, in the 1970s and the 1980s, it more or less died, and now students are apathetic. First of all, that's absolutely untrue. The major popular movements that have had a longstanding effect on the society and on the world are movements of the 1970s and the 1980s. The women's movement, the environmental movement, the Third World solidarity movements, these developed after the 1960s, after the collapse of the sixties movements.

But they were not primarily student movements. In fact they sank much deeper roots into U.S. society. So compare the solidarity movements with Central America in the 1980s with the anti-Vietnam War movement of the 1960s. Well, they're strikingly different. The anti-Vietnam War movement of the 1960s was really largely a student movement, and while it did very courageous and important things, it was quite restricted. So, for example, in the 1960s it never occurred to anybody in their wildest imagination to go to live in a Vietnamese village in the hope that a white face might cut down the level of state terrorism. That was inconceivable. But as you know, thousands of Americans did that in the 1980s. The solidarity movements were much more widespread and much more deeply rooted in American society. They were coming right out of Main Street, in fact, often from conservative religious circles, like Witness For Peace. They were involved in development. People involved themselves directly in the lives of the victims and, on an enormous scale, resisted the U.S.-run violence. The United States was never able to invade Central America the way it invaded South Vietnam, because there was just far too much domestic resistance.

I think an accurate picture would be that the movements grew and developed in the 1970s and more in the 1980s, and became far more deeply integrated into the core of American society. Now, new developments are taking place. For example, the labor movement is undergoing a period of revitalization with lots of interaction with people in other sectors of society, including the universities. That's a very positive development. Also cross-border interactions — concern within the American labor movement for the conditions of work and the state of working people in other countries. That's new. The bureaucracy of the labor movement had been working hand in hand with the state executive to undermine unions since World War II. That has changed. These changes come from changes at the grassroots level. Where they will go, who knows. But there are many very hopeful signs.

ENDNOTES

Preface
1 James Peck (ed), *The Chomsky Reader*, Pantheon Books, 1987, 320.
2 Jethro Pettit of Oxfam's Latin America desk, quoted in Peck (ed) *The Chomsky Reader*, 320–21.
3 Interview with Noam Chomsky, this book, Ch. 3, 53.
4 Peck (ed), *The Chomsky Reader*, 321.
5 Milan Rai, *Chomsky's Politics*, Verso, 1995, 153.
6 See Edward S Herman and Noam Chomsky, *Manufacturing Consent: The Political Economy of the Mass Media*, Vintage, 1994; and Noam Chomsky, *Necessary Illusions: Thought Control in Democratic Societies*, Pluto Press, 1989.
7 Rai, *Chomsky's Politics*, 38.
8 See Herman and Chomsky, *Manufacturing Consent*, Ch. 3.
9 Interview with Noam Chomsky, this book, Ch. 3, 45.
10 The afternoon lectures, which focused on contemporary political issues, were subsequently published as: *On Power and Ideology: The Managua Lectures*, South End Press, 1987.
11 Chomsky, *On Power and Ideology*, 5.
12 Chomsky, *On Power and Ideology*, 6–7.
13 Quoted in Rai, *Chomsky's Politics*, 153.
14 Noam Chomsky interviewed by David Barsamian, *The Common Good*, Odonian Press, 1998, 158.

Chapter 1: 1492: The First Invasion of Globalization
1 Quoted in Noam Chomsky, *Year 501: The Conquest Continues*, Verso, 1993, 4.
2 Las Casas published an eyewitness description of the "Destruction of the Indies" in 1552, quoted in Chomsky, *Year 501*, 32.
3 Quoted in Chomsky, *On Power and Ideology*, 8.
4 U.S. Ambassador to the UN, 1981–85.
5 U.S. Secretary of State, 1982–89.
6 U.S. Assistant Secretary of State for Human Rights and Humanitarian Affairs, 1981–85; Assistant Secretary of State for Inter-American Affairs, 1985–89.

Chapter 2: Latin America and the Vietnam War Syndrome
1 Quoted in Chomsky, *On Power and Ideology*, 15–16.
2 Ibid, 16.
3 Ibid, 59.
4 Ibid, 108.
5 U.S. State Department paper released in 1981, alleging heavy Soviet

support to El Salvador's guerrillas and later found to have been based on false documentation.
6 U.S. Ambassador to the UN, 1961–65.
7 Elected president of Guatemala, 1951–54.
8 Elected president of Guatemala, 1945–51.
9 U.S.-installed dictator, 1930–61.

Chapter 3: The United States: The Superpower That is Afraid of Small Countries
1 Quoted in Chomsky, *Year 501*, 142.
2 Quoted in Chomsky, *On Power and Ideology*, 3.
3 Quoted in Chomsky, *Year 501*, 34.
4 Quoted in Chomsky, *On Power and Ideology*, 85.
5 Conservative think-tank founded in 1973; especially influential during the Reagan and Bush years.
6 Daniel Moynihan was U.S. Ambassador to the UN in 1975 and became Senator (R) in 1976.

Chapter 4: Washington: The Principal Terrorist Government in the World
1 Quoted in Chomsky, *Year 501*, 29.
2 Quoted in Noam Chomsky and Edward S Herman, *The Washington Connection and Third World Fascism: The Political Economy of Human Rights Volume I*, Hale & Iremonger, 1980, 100.
3 Quoted in Chomsky, *On Power and Ideology*, 14.

Chapter 5: Irangate: Trading with the Enemy
1 Quoted in Chomsky, *On Power and Ideology*, 38.
2 U.S. National Security Adviser, 1983–85; one of three National Security Council officials charged in the Iran-Contra hearings.
3 Report of the investigation of the National Security Council's role in the Iran-Contra affair, commissioned by Reagan after the diversion of funds to the Contras was disclosed and headed by former Senator John Tower. The Report concluded that the Iran-Contra scandal was a result of the failure of the White House officials to follow procedures.
4 National Security Council aide, 1981–86; found guilty in 1989 on three charges for his role in covering up the Iran-Contra affair.

Chapter 6: Cuba: "Ripe for the Picking" by the United States
1 Quoted in Chomsky, *Year 501*, 37.
2 Quoted in Chomsky, *On Power and Ideology*, 36.
3 Quoted in Peck (ed), *The Chomsky Reader*, 360–61.
4 Simón Bolívar was known as "the Liberator" for his leading role in South American independence from Spain.

Chapter 7: The United States and the Future of Cuba
1 Quoted in Chomsky, *Year 501*, 143.
2 Ibid, 215.
3 Ibid, 217.
4 Quoted in Noam Chomsky, *Deterring Democracy*, Verso, 1991, 296.

Chapter 8: The Future of the Third World
1 Quoted in Noam Chomsky, *World Orders Old and New*, Columbia University Press, 1994, 179.
2 Ibid, 181.
3 Formed in 1975, the "Group of Seven" (United States, Japan, Canada, Italy, Great Britain, France, Germany) coordinates macro-economic and international policies.
4 The General Agreement on Tariffs and Trade has been a mechanism for coordinating trade policies since 1948. GATT was integrated into the World Trade Organization when that body was formed in 1995.

Chapter 9: The Global Society
1 Quoted in Chomsky, *Deterring Democracy*, 29.
2 Quoted in Chomsky, *World Orders Old and New*, 71.

Chapter 10: Mexico: Between NAFTA and the Zapatistas
1 Quoted in Chomsky, *Year 501*, 38.
2 Ibid, 99.
3 U.S. Secretary of Defense, 1981–89.

Chapter 11: The Pope and the Asian Crisis
1 Quoted in Chomsky, *On Power and Ideology*, 71.

REBEL LIVES
A new series from Ocean Press

I WAS NEVER ALONE
A Prison Diary from El Salvador
By *Nidia Díaz*
Nidia Díaz (born María Marta Valladares) gives a dramatic and inspiring personal account of her experience as a guerrilla commander during El Salvador's civil war. Seriously wounded, she was captured in combat by Cuban-exile CIA agent Félix Rodríguez. Nidia Díaz was the FMLN's Vice-Presidential candidate in 1999.
ISBN 1-876175-17-6

PRIEST AND PARTISAN
A South African Journey of Father Michael Lapsley
By *Michael Worsnip*
The story of Father Michael Lapsley, an anti-apartheid priest, and how he survived a South African letter bomb attack in 1990 in which he lost both hands and an eye.
Foreword by Nelson Mandela
ISBN 1-875284-96-6

SLOVO
The Unfinished Autobiography of ANC Leader Joe Slovo
A revealing and highly entertaining autobiography of one of the key figures of South Africa's African National Congress. As an immigrant, a Jew, a communist, a guerrilla fighter and political strategist — and white — few public figures in South Africa were as demonized by the apartheid government as Joe Slovo.
Introduction by Nelson Mandela.
ISBN 1-875284-95-8

MY EARLY YEARS
By *Fidel Castro*
In the twilight of his life, Fidel Castro, one of the century's most controversial figures, reflects on his childhood, youth and student days. In an unprecedented and remarkably candid manner, the Cuban leader describes his family background and the religious and moral influences that led to his early involvement in politics.
Introductory essay by Gabriel García Márquez
ISBN 1-876175-07-9

Also from Ocean Press

JOSE MARTI READER
Writings on the Americas
This Reader presents an outstanding new anthology of the writings, letters and poetry of José Martí—one of the most brilliant and impassioned Latin American intellectuals of the 19th century.
ISBN 1-875284-12-5

FIDEL CASTRO READER
The voice of one of the 20th century's most controversial political figures — as well as one of the world's greatest orators — is captured in this new selection of Castro's key speeches over 40 years.
ISBN 1-876175-11-7

CUBAN REVOLUTION READER
A Documentary History
Edited by Julio García Luis
An outstanding anthology documenting the past four decades of Cuban history. This Reader presents a comprehensive overview of the key moments in the Cuban Revolution.
ISBN 1-876175-10-9

CUBA AND THE UNITED STATES
A Chronological History
By Jane Franklin
Based on exceptionally wide research, this updated and expanded chronology relates day by day, year by year, the developments involving the two neighboring countries from the 1959 Cuban revolution through 1995.
ISBN 1-875284-92-3

PSYWAR ON CUBA
The Declassified History of U.S. Anti-Castro Propaganda
Edited by Jon Elliston
Newly declassified CIA and U.S. Government documents are reproduced here, with extensive commentary providing the history of Washington's 40-year campaign of psychological warfare and propaganda to destabilize Cuba and undermine its revolution.
ISBN 1-876175-09-5

AFTER MORUROA
France in the South Pacific
By Nic Maclellan and Jean Chesneaux
"This book outlines the history of French colonialism in the South Pacific and shows how Pacific peoples are seeking to determine their own future, in freedom and dignity."
José Ramos Horta, East Timorese Nobel Peace Prize Co-laureate
ISBN 1-876175-05-2

AFROCUBA
An Anthology of Cuban Writing on Race, Politics and Culture
Edited by Pedro Pérez Sarduy and Jean Stubbs
What is it like to be Black in Cuba? Does racism exist in a revolutionary society that claims to have abolished it? How does the legacy of slavery and segregation live on in today's Cuba? *AfroCuba* looks at the Black experience in Cuba through the eyes of the island's writers, scholars and artists.
ISBN 1-875284-41-9

BAY OF PIGS AND THE CIA
Cuban Secret Files Reveal the Story Behind the Invasion
By Juan Carlos Rodríguez
No CIA document or other account of the mercenary invasion of Cuba in 1961 can be read in the same way after the publication of Cuba's story of the Bay of Pigs and its aftermath.
ISBN 1-875284-98-2

CUBA: TALKING ABOUT REVOLUTION
Conversations with Juan Antonio Blanco by Medea Benjamin
A frank discussion on the current situation in Cuba, this book presents an all-too-rare opportunity to hear the voice of one of the island's leading intellectuals. This new edition features a new essay by Blanco, "Cuba: 'socialist museum' or social laboratory?"
ISBN 1-875284-97-7

DEADLY DECEITS
My 25 Years in the CIA
By Ralph W. McGehee
A new, updated edition of this classic account of the CIA's deeds and deceptions by one of its formerly most prized recruits.
ISBN 1-876175-19-2

Che Guevara titles from Ocean Press

CHE GUEVARA READER
Writings on Guerrilla Strategy, Politics and Revolution
Edited by David Deutschmann
Three decades after the death of the legendary Latin American figure, this book presents the most comprehensive selection of Guevara's writings ever to be published in English.
ISBN 1-875284-93-1

CHE IN AFRICA
Che Guevara's Congo diary
By William Gálvez
Che Guevara disappeared from Cuba in 1965 to lead a guerrilla mission to Africa in support of liberation movements. Considerable speculation has always surrounded Guevara's departure from Cuba and why he went to fight in Africa. *Che in Africa* is the previously untold story of Che Guevara's "lost year" in Africa.
ISBN 1-876175-08-7

CHE GUEVARA AND THE FBI
U.S. Political Police Dossier on the Latin American Revolutionary
Edited by Michael Ratner and Michael Steven Smith
Thirty years after the death of Che Guevara, a Freedom of Information case has succeeded in obtaining the FBI and CIA files on Che Guevara.
ISBN 1-875284-76-1

CHE — A MEMOIR BY FIDEL CASTRO
Preface by Jesús Montané
Edited by David Deutschmann
For the first time Fidel Castro writes with candor and affection of his relationship with Ernesto Che Guevara, documenting his extraordinary bond with Cuba from the revolution's early days to the final guerrilla expeditions to Africa and Bolivia.
ISBN 1-875284-15-X

Ocean Press, GPO Box 3279, Melbourne 3001, Australia
● Fax: 61-3-9372 1765 ● E-mail: ocean_press@msn.com.au

Ocean Press, PO Box 834, Hoboken, NJ 07030, USA
● Fax: 1-201-617 0203